J. EVETTS HALEY

~

AND THE PASSING
OF THE OLD WEST

J. EVETTS HALEY

AND THE
PASSING OF THE
OLD WEST

*A Bibliography of His Writings, with a
Collection of Essays upon His Character,
Genius, Personality, Skills, and
Accomplishments.*

Compiled and Edited By
Chandler A. Robinson

Jenkins Publishing Company
Austin, Texas 1978

Designed by
Larry Smitherman

Library of Congress Catalogue No. 78-61170
I.S.B.N. 0-8363-0160-9

CONTENTS

PREFACE

some words from and about my father

by Evetts Haley Jr.

Putting words on paper about one of the greatest writers, storytellers and Southwestern characters of his time is a tough task for any of that individual's devoted and admiring readers. It is no less so for his son. The dates and titles covering fifty or more years appearing in a bibliography of J. Evetts Haley adequately attest to the importance of the career of the man, both as an historian, and as a patriot.

The wide diversity of people invited to contribute to Chandler Robinson's second bibliography of J. Evetts Haley further attests to the remarkably varied interests of the man, who more than any other of my own acquaintance, will leave an indelible brand on more than half a century of recent Texas and Southwestern history. His influence has been memorable on so many people, both those who have gone before, and, more significantly, those who will survive beyond.

But aside from his historical and patriotic activities, the most compelling of the emotions and the most intense of the

7

powers of concentration of J. Evetts Haley as a man, have been consistently dedicated to the development of the character within his family, to the preservation of honor for the Haley name, and to attention to the detail, however mundane, necessary for the maintenance of an independent posture in personal and family business, in spite of all adversity, natural and otherwise. And in this order he has devoted his time and energies. Literary and other pursuits have always been allotted his time on a secondary basis. Yet, unlike many of his contemporaries in the literary field, he has never been charged with the production of a literary work of secondary importance or quality.

It is likely that more distant observers and historians of the future would, in the treatise of a son on a public spirited father, find more to their benefit information of an intimate and specifically personal nature rather than another general discussion of the work of a man recognized in his own time as an authentic historian and writer of tremendous style. For those of us nearest to my father, through half or more of his nearly seventy-five years of intense pursuit of his varied interests, reflection echoes repeated emphasis on his absolute self-discipline.

His basic nature is such that the obvious self-indulgence of others in everyday habits has always been an easy source of irritation to him. But when these traits have happened to appear in a colleague or acquaintance, the passage of time has always tended to relax him. All those J. Evetts Haley thinks to be miscreants at one time or another may redeem themselves later through the obvious use of good judgment and steadfastness during conflicts of principle.

For the sake of illustration, had J. Evetts Haley been a contemporary of Patrick Henry, and if the latter were the playboy that some historians are fond of claiming he was, dad would have had little patience with him prior to the emotional speech he delivered before the Virginia House of Delegates. But following that memorable performance, J. Evetts would have been Patrick's devoted admirer and colleague.

Pursuing this type of illustration a bit further, although both Washington and Jefferson were men of affairs and property, and great patriots, both of whom my father greatly admires, the typical reader and observer would probably associate dad and his tendencies closest to Jefferson, the thinker and writer. If so, they would be mistaken. Dad is the fonder of Washington, the doer, the fighter, the man of great self-denial, the man without personal or family complications throughout his varied career.

After George Washington, the figures my father admires most from American history are Robert E. Lee and Douglas MacArthur. From the more strictly political scene, he has pointed to James Madison and James Monroe. And from more recent history, he admires that great Democrat, Grover Cleveland, and the great Republican, Robert A. Taft, the elder. Thus, he has usually pointed to those men who were more renowned for their courage in the face of adversity, rather than the noted thinkers who have left behind academic and even scholarly writings, as good historical candidates to be our family heroes.

But in life there seem always to be exceptions. The exception to dad's usual lack of affinity for fiction, especially modern fiction, is the Bard of Avon, William Shakespeare. Most of dad's cow country friends have never heard him do so, but he is capable of quoting at length several of the great tragedies. Little do many friends realize that he places stock in many, many lessons on human character and behavior found in the lines of these plays. Dad considers Shakespeare one of the greatest philosophers and storytellers of all time, and the greatest master of the English language.

Something he seldom admits to his friends is his love for the English language and the proper use thereof. Frequently, with passing years, he has delighted in abusing the grammar here and there, the more so in ranch type conversation, (and he doesn't much enjoy any that isn't ranch type, wherever the location). Sometimes he is even irritated when some family member good-naturedly corrects him. On the other hand, he has no patience with pseudo-sophisticated bankers, reporters, and slick admen, probably all with degrees from some state university or college, who persist in making the noun 'loan' into a verb.

On the subject of language and verbs, he has frequently told me, "write like you talk, and talk like a cowpuncher

9

walks," by using short choppy sentences and vigorous, active verbs. When editing copy written by others, he makes his blue pencil most destructive of useless adjectives and prepositional phrases. He feels that one adjective is apt to be better than another, one is surely better than two, and none might be better than one. Even though many of his sentences are long and involved, they do seem to flow, and unlike many writers with less talent and discipline, he is capable of logically defending his use of every word.

To illustrate, he might have written the preceding paragraph as follows: "Use direct language. Write like you talk. Talk like a cowpuncher walks. Use short, choppy sentences. Write with vigorous, active verbs. Shun useless adjectives and phrases." His own longer, more involved sentences are still lucid and logical. The careful reader will understand and appreciate his discriminating use of descriptive words. To those less disciplined and experienced writers, he would say, "You don't work hard enough with a blue pencil!"

If there is any one glaring contradiction to J. Evett's approach to the varied work in his life, it is in his use of time, and his concept of its appropriate expenditure. He doesn't have time to wait for fish to bite. He seldom has time to wait for a flight of doves to come by. He has no time to watch a football game, even on television; although, at one time, he enjoyed fishing, hunting, and football as sports. He is a strong believer in good manners and common courtesy, (I have never heard him use any of the usual four letter expletives other than 'damn' or 'hell'), but he has little time for social affairs, such as formal dinners and cocktail parties, and no time for cards, dances, music or television. He rushes at everything he does as if the whole of the time he spends at it is near a complete waste, with only two possible exceptions.

Dad's first extravagance with time is in conversation and reminiscing, especially with old-timers from the Southwest or ingenious movers in the field of business or property management, be they humble or be they renowned. Dad's second inclination to use time patiently and liberally is in the handling of cattle. "You can't put a cow through a gate until she sees it." There are times when cattle should be crowded, but there are others when they can't be, without a cowboy causing himself and his crew trouble and a lot of extra work. Persons without any experience in working cattle are probably incapable of appreciating this. And even some people who have spent most of their life-times around cattle either do not understand or do not appreciate the finer point involved here.

But of all the persons with whom I have had the experience of working cattle, although there are two with whom I had just as soon work, there are none superior to J. Evetts Haley as a *cowman*. He knows what a cow is thinking before she thinks. He is a skilled judge of their condition — he can ride through a herd of cows and within a few minutes point out every cow which is "not doing what she ought to" and every one which is "on the mend," or improving over the average of the whole herd. In more than thirty years of working on horseback and with cattle, almost daily I have seen dad impatient with progress, and many times mad enough, I thought, to have a stroke, but never have I seen him, in anger, kill or injure any animal. And judging by his example having so seldom seen him whip or even poke a cow, I wonder how the term 'cowpoke' ever took root. For years I can remember seeing dad primarily use the flat of his hand in a loud slap on the flat of the animal's hip as his principal means of getting movement. In a chute anyone is apt to have to poke cattle and dad is no exception, but he never uses or permits anyone else the use of a steel bar or piece of pipe as poker in a chute on his outfit. To appreciative readers of the *XIT, Milton, Goodnight, Littlefield,* or *Heraldry of the Range* books, it is worth pointing out that he wrote well on these subjects not so much because he had earned a Masters Degree in History at the University of Texas, but more because he understood the action he chronicled from his own range experiences.

There may be a strong correlation between the ability of the historical writer to entertain his readers and the raconteur to attract and entertain an audience. Not every good storyteller is able to thread the history of a ranch or the biography of a pioneer cowman on to the pages of a manuscript.

Through the last fifty years, hundreds of volumes have been written by distinguished professors of history at famous universities. Some of these were diligently researched and honestly and mechanically well-written, and some are seldom read, except when assigned to students by the professors who wrote them.

Most any reader of the Goodnight book will understand the following premise. The proof of the style of J. Evetts Haley is that his books are read over and over by people who are not at all interested in the minute factual detail of an episode in history, even though that detail is there in abundance. His books are also read by people who simply want to relax and be entertained. Few historical writers today meet the factual and mechanical criteria while at the same time entertaining the typical reader as does J. Evetts Haley.

With passing time it has become apparent to those closest to my father that it is easier for him to recount his experiences and stories orally to a group, than it is to face up to the typewriter and a blank sheet of paper. Now though, he seldom "limbers up" except in the company of men with a ready sense of humor and a facility as good listeners. His apparent reluctance to engage in competition as a raconteur is not due to even a touch of arrogance. With increasing age, the necessary energy for animated conversation is present only in conjunction with keen interest in subject matter, and the subject matter is rarely sufficiently stimulating when its choice is not pretty much under his own conversational control.

Now here is an attempt at an analogy. In the professional pursuit of writing, those who are trained first and become disciplined while making their living as journalistic writers — that is for newspapers, magazines, radio or TV scripts — will never be the same kind of writers of books as those who have pursued narrative writing in book form from the beginning of their careers. Many times dad has been heard to observe that those with journalistic training become lost in their material when attempting to write books. He says the job of organization of their subject matter throws them. This must have its deleterious effect, but there is another significant difference: the freedom of choice of subject matter during the writer's formative years.

The writer who launches his career primarily as an historian does not have to write the story of the Inca civilization for his first book, if he finds the nineteenth century exploits of the Plains Comanches more of a challenge. And he does not have to concentrate on the effect the Comanches had on the frontier development of the Southwest, if he finds the action on the great cattle trails more to his liking. The point is, my father chooses his own subject matter nearly always from the raw material of his career, (since he does not, and a truly conscientious historian usually can not, make a living from his writing anyway) while the journalist has his subjects chosen for him, if not by his editor, then by the progress of current events beyond his control.

Therein may lie a clue to the interest of the historical writer who is almost equally noted as a raconteur. Having control of the topic before the house is a lifetime habit. When it happens that some in a group capture the floor for a discussion of any sort of athletic event or hunting or fishing or other "vacation" type of activity, dad decides that it is past his bedtime.

There has been so much attention given the activities and involvement of J. Evetts Haley in the political sphere that unfortunately, to the general public, this may be the best known aspect of his career. Perhaps little can be added here to the published record that would be of interest to future historians.

But something is going to be said anyway. Dad is a student of the great Irish philosopher, Edmund Burke, and probably has been heard to quote him in speeches of a political nature more than any other political theorist. Burke's admonition that in the course of political affairs, "the only thing necessary for the triumph of evil is for good men to do nothing" has been a favorite quotation of his.

Although dad is widely known among his colleagues as an apt and devoted student of Edmund Burke, Thomas Jefferson, William Graham Sumner, Guglielmo Ferrero, Oswald Spengler, Ludwig Von Mises, Wilhelm Roepke, Kuehnelt-Leddihn and Ortega y Gasset, many of his readers of frontier range history are unaware that he is an original thinker in the field of the philosophy of liberty. Unlike some of his contemporaries among modern libertarians and others often branded "right-wingers" by the liberal American news media, he has through the years developed ability as a tactician.

Some of the libertarian apostles of this generation have great difficulty reconciling the pursuits of liberty with the practical pursuit of American politics. Undeniably a considerable contradiction is ever present between the two. But to deny that an accommodation is possible, is to deny that the Constitutional system of the American Republic is workable. And to propose a return to a governing system of monarchy or right-wing dictatorship today, would be to promote a further reaction in the public toward the oppressive tyranny of the left-wing masses and communism.

In September, 1975, J. Evetts wrote a letter to an English professor at the University of Dallas in which he expressed his diappointment that the conservatives in American politics have been unable to coalesce on tactics. He wrote, "The 100% conservatives, largely our kind of die-hards, will never, of course, get their perfect man. In fact there was only One and he was nailed to the cross two thousand years ago. My old friend, Ortega y Gasset, long ago pointed out one of the cardinal rules that every conservative should observe, 'The first principle in politics is to exclude all excluding.' We need all of the honest help we can get from any source in this vital fight; no matter wherever the individual has been in the past, we should and must welcome it."

Even so, the tactics often proposed by J. Evetts Haley to many functionaries soliciting support for candidates for officers from County Commissioner to President, have unfortunately been too straight forward and tough-minded to be appreciated for their intrinsic merit. But some of the simple newspaper ad-copy written by J. Evetts for various local causes has been classic. And some of it has had an obvious effect on election day.

Although J. Evetts Haley seems to intuitively like men who are blacksmiths and does not hesitate to use that good old English term 'smith' to describe a real craftsman in metals, I have never heard him say so, but I know instinctively that he would not approve of the term 'wordsmith.' At the risk of incurring his undying displeasure therefore, I am going to describe my father as a superb wordsmith. I find the term aptly descriptive of the art and craft practiced by J. Evetts Haley.

I will perhaps remember him best for his flowing prose. Particularly meaningful to me are some passages that I quote here. In appreciation of his work I am in the same realm as any

14

of his readers, though I have been close to him as his son for more than forty years, and business partner for twenty-four years. At the reader's trough only the blind or unemotional are at a loss. All others belly up on an equal footing.

"What handsome and unexpected dividends a cowboy's life can pay . . . ," and also from *A Day with Dan Casement*, ". . . while the cocker left us to follow his sensitive nose in search of Nature's wonders daily rejuvenated in the growth of the yard. Meanwhile, the master of the house, with violent feeling and an occasional tear, read aloud Kipling's warning to human weaklings who disregard the lessons that the cocker read so clearly."

In a few well-chosen words, this paragraph illustrates dad's complete ease and joy with his own station in life. It tells me what an able and sensitive naturalist he is. It is also indicative of his ingrained sense of propriety. It tells me of his deeply emotional nature. It verifies for me that he is a very literary person. It also exemplifies his pride in racial heritage and in human character (and the two go together). It says something, too, of his abiding patriotism.

". . . I recall following my Mother to our dobie barn behind our old home in Midland, Texas, where, with gentle head pressed in Brownie's flank, she squeezed my tin cup full. Then, nose in foam, it was my delight to drink it down still warm and homogenized by animal nature, a soothing fluid to sensitive stomachs."

From *A Bit of Bragging About a Cow*, (included with *The Heraldry of the Range* and *Ode to Nita* as my personal favorites of his prose works), the quoted paragraph tells me nearly all that I need to know to tell my children about their grandather's raising, his loving relationship with their great grandmother, and the importance of a cow to their own survival during times of scarcity and famine, which may at some point come to America too!

Another of the interesting facets of the character and career of J. Evetts Haley, especially by comparison to those of other men, is the limited number of persons who have had a deep and lasting influence on his life and views. My mother commented to me on this anomaly. It was her observation that probably fewer than five people had such an influence. She mentioned his mother, Julia Evetts Haley, as paramount among those who did. She also observed that, in the field of history, Dr. E.C. Barker, Professor and Head of the Department of History at the University of Texas, and in the field of business, L.L. Dent of Dallas, a friend and one time employer, both had lasting influence. It was my observation that my mother, Mary Vernita Stewart Haley, also made an indelible impression on his philosophy, character and life. But back to the illustrations from a wordsmith!

"The cow to which I propose a monument established no bloodlines, set no butter-fat records, and produced no prize winning beeves for the International Show. But she did take care of herself and her calf out on the open range of Texas." Also from *A Bit of Bragging About a Cow*, this is a monumental line and I hope to live to see it in bronze on the base of a monument to "Old Maude" and the range Longhorn in general, and erected on the grounds of the library and history center bearing dad's and mother's name in Midland, Texas. These lines tell me something about the fierceness of dad's appreciation for self-reliance. They also remind me of his great sense of humor and perspective, and how dad has often admonished me that a man will not have much of the latter, who doesn't have a healthy amount of the former.

"Distinguished Guests, Mr. Davenport, President Rainey, Members of the Association, and my little boy, Jimmie:" —

This salutation from the "Eugene Barker Portrait Presentation" before the Texas and Southwestern Historical Society (and later published in its quarterly) reflects both public and very personal love and respect of a father for his son. It came when I was barely eleven years old. I have never forgotten it and what it meant to me. And I never will.

"When I left the short-grass ranges of western Texas to sample the easy grace of life in Austin . . . ," also from the Barker Portrait Presentation speech, reminds me of the tremendous energy and vitality of my father. It also reminds me of his wide variety of interests in life and life-styles, and his great appreciation of many of their differences.

"Barely more than one hundred years ago differences over vital issues precipitated our land and people into strife and turmoil. Hot-blooded men, having failed to compose those differences on the deliberative level, joined them on the field of conflict in the War Between the States, where they were destined to be settled by superior force, rather than by moral principle."

These lines from "John R. Baylor, Irrepressible Rebel," included in *Men of Fiber*, remind me of two things that I want to impress upon all my children and my sons in particular. The first is that they are great grandsons of the Old South and they should always remember and be proud of the traditions and heritage that have been left to them as a result. The second is that the first great abrogation of the United States Constitution came with the War Between the States, and that the big lesson to be remembered from that is that wars are never decisive in behalf of morals. They only decide who has the greatest firepower.

Also, writing about circuit riders in *Men of Fiber*, "Those bygone Christian advocates, sitting resolutely in their saddles, came to occupy a mighty place in the lives of lonely Americans far from the graces of cultivated life and the comforting sanctuary of churches. They carried 'the Word' to the far frontiers with the dedication and sacrifice — the force and conviction — that rides alone with those who truly believe." This passage, from "Andrew Jackson Potter, Fighting Parson," will always remind me what a deeply God-fearing man my father is, and what a disciple of dedication and self-sacrifice he has been.

Taken from *Then Came Christmas for Mildred Taitt*, these lines ring to me the faith and conviction I have seen in my father: "Despite the clouds of gloom throughout the world, we in this country still believe in the spirit of Christmas. We believe that men of gallantry, nobility and courage will again rise up and take the saddle. The history of our land and the traditions of our fathers confirm us in this conclusion." These are indicative of the faith of a father who became a non-church goer as a young man, because he early saw the Methodist Church departing from the Bible in favor of the "social" or socialist message.

". . . When we consider the wide range of action, and the vivid and almost infinite variety of subject matter that invited attention, it is not altogether surprising that historians and critics have sometimes ridden laggard horses." This observation, from *Frank Reaugh, Man and Artist*, serves to remind me not only of dad's tremendous appreciation of art, but also of his critical ability to look back over his shoulder and question the competence of his profession in general and himself in particular. This critical ability has been the hallmark not only of his pursuit of history, but also of his pursuit of a living in the cow business.

But, again on art, "Whatever the changing conception of the ephemeral moment, the capricious whims of the public, the weird cults of the phoney, or the pretensions of the avaricious dealer, genuine art is untouched and eternal. For art, that finest expression of man's timeless groping for lovely form and color, for spirit and beauty, ethereally fixed by paint on canvas, is for the ages."

And finally on art, "For, as irrefutably written in history, when night settles over the world and all seems lost, art survives, a celestial benediction glowing in the darkness." Taken from *A Cowman's Comment on Art*, written for and published by my wife, Frances, and me, these lines remind me of my father's wholesome purity of taste, and also of his fundamental nature. He places this form of man's production above the crass and material.

It has often been said that the true test of a writer of prose or lyrics is contained in the question supposedly asked of the literary giant, Guy de Maupassant. "You writers always tell of people and their emotions such as jealousy, greed, love and hate. Why don't you show how you can write by making your subject an inanimate object?" So de Maupassant wrote "The Piece of String."

I will always remember my father writing about an object, too, *The Alamo Mission Bell*, and hear this line ringing in my subconcious: "This bell had for a long time sounded the sacred vespers, calling the faithful to prayer and confession, at that hallowed mission, no matter anyone's religion, which had become the cradle of Texas independence and freedom — the Alamo."

Speaking of the Alamo, dad has a favorite and frequently uttered admonition; he says, "When you start to the Alamo, there is no turning back." As a patriotic venture among the political crusades of his career, Dad fully believed that he was on the way to his Alamo in 1964 when he wrote a little book called *A Texan Looks at Lyndon.* He wrote it in five months. That's faster than he wrote some individual chapters of the Goodnight and Milton books. The task exhausted him emotionally and came near killing him physically.

Dad found, to his surprise, that he had written a bestseller and the first and only book of his career that really made money. Surely the Lord smiled, as hundreds of thousands of American activists rushed to buy copies by the tens and even by the hundreds to read and distribute. "To those who seek the truth and love liberty, and are willing to struggle to find the one, and fight to hold the other," were the dedicatory lines in the book.

Fortunately, the publication of "that book" did not conclude the literary and historical career of J. Evetts Haley. Several significant works have been produced since, in spite of his long absence from the typewriter following its publication. Unfortunately, it seems to me, a great many collectors, critics, and would-be historians, among them some close friends, prefer to dismiss from their minds *A Texan Looks at Lyndon,* even as the contemporaries of Charles Dickens might have dismissed a book entitled *Let Us Not Elect John Bull Prime Minister,* had he written such a book.

If I have any statement of opinion on the work of my father worthy of emphasis, it is this: more welders, mechanics, truck drivers, painters, plumbers, policemen, preachers, and typical barflies read and absorbed "that book" than all his other put together, many times over. Probably more of the world's conscientious historians and commentators of the coming centuries will read and ponder *A Texas Looks at Lyndon* than all his other books put together. In a way, it is of the stuff and something of the sense of prophesy that causes many students today to remember the historian Gibbon.

But for me, the son of a noted father and a great and patient mother, the lines that throughout my life shall define that goal ever to be sought in personal conduct, but never quite reached, appear in *Ode to Nita:* "The gentle Mary Stuart, Queen of Scots, at her best in royal robes, could not have surpassed in proud demeanor and natural dignity my own Mary Vernita Stewart, whose royal plaid was traced in calico as the born queen of my remote and menial cowcamps." And I will remember what moved my father the most and matured me in an atmosphere at home of mutual respect, ". . . my dear grey-gowned Nita — who really played the leading part, sat far back in the wings of life, and with vast pride and infinite patience, wove all the cloth for me to wear."

Just as he has written that "The beginning of brands is almost lost in antiquity, though in the Southwest the practice came up the trail with Longhorn herds from Mexico. . . . But the Anglo-Saxons, with their genius for simplicity, discarded the intricate and ornate symbols that marred the hides of scrawny herds and adopted characters of their own," and "Great range enterprises and institutions, conceived and carried to immense proportions by bold and able men, were known by their brands," so it seems that this range historian, sadly, perhaps one of the last of the great Anglo-Saxons, will also leave a special brand on posterity. That mark will be his stirring and distinctive use of words. Words that express deep and exciting emotions — words distilled from his tireless research, necessary to the transmittal of history into the beautiful English language, in a way, I believe, that assures the recollections of my father as the wordsmith of the West Texas Ranges.

And finally I quote what I believe will be classic lines for posterity, and another nomination of mine for a bronze plaque to be erected on a lonesome, windswept, forever unplowed prairie: "The old world had its armorial patterns — its coats of arms embroidered in its banners and embossed upon its shields — the marks of chivalry at home and daring in the field. The silversmiths had their hallmarks, which are still standing guarantees of supreme artistry and skill. The grandees of once great and gracious Spain had their rubrics — the distinctive flourishes with which they signed their names. But the Western World has its brands — the heraldry of the range."

This medley of lines, from the pages of J. Evetts Haley, provides in great measure the heraldry of a range writer for his ranch-raised son.

1

J. EVETTS HALEY
AND THE PASSING
OF THE OLD WEST

by Chandler A. Robinson

Reliving more than sixty productive years in the breaks and plains of West Texas, Evetts Haley must surely be filled with varied emotions about places, things, events and people long since "passed over the range;" of dreary days with trail herds, still drearier nights guarding restless cattle on the bed grounds; of blinding winter storms and stifling summer heat waves. As a young cowboy in those early days he undoubtedly preferred to move from place to place in the saddle, scorning any manual labor but that of the round-up, looking with disdain upon the farmer, the nester and the sheep man.

Times changed and the change came slowly, evolutionary, material rather than physical. The barbed wire fence did more to bring it about than any other one thing. Evetts appeared on the scene just as the "old-timers" were phasing out, not by choice but by circumstance. Those vigorous individualists with their high-heeled boots not built for hard work on the ground, with spurs they hated to remove even to attend the shindigs in the schoolhouse, found themselves sadly hampered and really outclassed at post-hole digging, hay making and such, to them, degrading labor.

Thus, Evetts became an eager observer of events as well as part of the change that witnessed the old-timer's place gradually taken by a new type of cowboy, who instead of boots more than likely wore flat-heeled shoes, who cast aside chaps for blue denim overalls — "Levis" from San Francisco. The old-timers grew up on the ranges and rode from infancy. The new cowboys were recruited from among the farmer boys who, during the branding season, worked on the range, and between times helped irrigate crops and put up hay for winter feeding.

When Evetts began his peregrinations accumulating artifacts and interviews of an earlier day, of the old-time type of cowboy, those who were in their prime in the years between 1880 and 1900, few were left.

A cowboy of that era, I am told, when he reached the age at which he could no longer ride a bucker and stay there, or flank a calf, became either a chamber-maid in some livery stable or a bartender.

Texas, at the time Evetts first set out in his tin lizzie — his wahoo — collecting "western artifacts," had more cattle than ever, but the old ranges had been cut up into fenced pastures. The range rider, carrying a few pounds of wire fence staples in his saddle pockets and a pair of fence pliers and a wire stretcher tied to his saddle, was a far more important personage then than the man who could once rope and tie down a steer in less than fifty seconds.

Evetts remembers that in the Southwest in Arizona, New Mexico, Southern Utah, Oklahoma and Texas there were still many good sized range cow outfits, and it was there you could find cowboys that ran fairly true to type. But there had been many changes.

As for myself, I make no claims to being a cowboy — far from it — but I was raised with horses, enjoyed considerable time on and with them as I grew up and, while strictly a "city feller," bunked for a spell on the HF Bar Ranch, spread over a wide expanse of the Big Horn mountains in Northern Wyoming, cut by the waters of Crazy Woman Creek, a tributary of Powder River. The nearest town was Buffalo, where I competed in that great and glorious event known as the "Buffalo, Wyo. Rodeo."

I, too, have seen a few changes. None of these present day men ride or handle the raw broncs with the recklessness, the tough, rough, wild-and-woolly manner displayed by the old-timers of Evetts' day, or the cowboys I can remember.

As for roping, that has become a lost art, except for the professionals in local rodeos and CRA sponsored events. But the pros of today wouldn't work ten days on a real cow ranch. During the period that Evetts was first earning his keep at range work, cows were worth about five dollars each and the owners did not particularly object to their men practicing on the stock, for without constant practice no man could hope to keep up his skill. But with rising prices and cows worth fifty dollars and up, practicing became an expensive affair for the owners. They raised serious objections to their men becoming expert ropers at such costs, for practice was to be had only with the range stock and that meant heavy losses in broken legs, horns, ribs and, often, necks.

Will Rogers, considered to be the greatest roper of them all, knew the value of constant practice. Of all the activities at his ranch in the hills above Santa Monica, California, he most enjoyed going out in the roping ring with the calves. There was always a small bunch of them on the place, kept for practice. Will's biographers have related that when he discovered that they became too tame after he had roped them again and again, he would ship them off and replace them with another lot that provided more sport.

I have been told that on a certain day in West Texas, Evetts and half a dozen punchers were riding toward the head-quarters ranch when across the road a string of cattle came trailing out from water. A high-headed steer stopped for a mo-ment, shook his head, sniffed at the men and then raced madly across the flat. Fourth of July was close at hand with roping matches in every little cow town in the country. Away went Evetts after him, untying his rope from the saddle and forming a loop as he rode. His moves were precise and calculated. Watching, you knew he'd done this many times before. Not far behind him trailed two others, eager to take their turn should Evetts "waste a loop."

Evetts practiced two distinct ways for roping a steer. "The first and most skillful," he explained to me one day as we rode in the breaks of his JH Ranch near Spearman," was by going over the withers. Then with a quick jerk the rope is pulled up around the front legs and the pony swung directly away from the steer. With the rope tied to the saddle horn the jerk at the other end sweeps the steer's legs out from under him and he is turned clear over, so stunned that there is little fight left in him. The pony, of course, knows his business and holds the rope taut while the rider, leaping from the saddle, quickly ties the fore feet and one hind foot closely together and the job is done. This method takes lots of practice. On the other hand, the ordinary, sure-fire method is to rope the steer by the horns, give the slack of the rope a sudden flip around the animal's rump just above the hocks and then, spurring the pony for a supreme effort, 'go yonderly' ahead and to the left, landing him all in a heap, generally with his head under his body in such a shape that it is almost impossible for him to get up."

As the use of barbed wire became more universal, Evetts watched as other pressures were brought to bear on the cowboy which limited his freedom of action and brought the sudden demise of the open range. There were the new laws, fostered by various societies for the prevention of cruelty to animals, forbidding roping practice on stock. Then they took away the sixshooter or "hog leg." Heavy penalties were enforced against the wearing of such "ornaments" in town or on the ranges. So, often as not, the weapon was hidden away in bed rolls, for a genuine cowboy couldn't imagine himself without his sixshooter somewhere near. Evetts never did part with his revolver, having it comfortably near, in the glove compartment of a car, in a brief case, suitcase or drawer, loaded and ready for use.

The happiness of the cowboy was further curtailed by the passage of laws against open gambling. Then, when the wave of prohibition swept across the range country from Canada to Mexico and the saloons were turned into ice cream parlors and soft drink emporiums, and they had to content themselves with lemonade, sassaparilla or the national beverage of Georgia, as Coca-Cola was called, they thought the world was coming to an end for sure, or to put it more succinctly, "Going to hell in an handbasket."

Shutting down of the open range not only caused the passing of the rugged old-time cowboy, but also of the Longhorn cattle, the maverick, and the rustler. In the place of the longhorns emerged great herds of fat cattle with blood in their veins the equal of any in the corn belt regions or their ancestors across the Atlantic. The cowboys who herded this gentler breed did so, not from the bucking broncs of earlier times, but more often from saddle horses with bloodlines flowing back to thoroughbreds who won Derbys. Instead of sixshooters they carried at the saddle horn a pair of fence pliers with a tobacco sack full of fence staples in saddle pockets where once a pint flask of red "licker" reposed.

The old-timer cowboy was picturesque and adventurous, but his successor became a better all around worker and a better citizen. The Haleys were deeply and actively involved in the development of West Texas. John Haley, Evetts' father, was an early day mayor of Midland and his mother a short-term president of Texas Technological College at Lubbock. Evetts, too, was always involved in civic, cultural, social and political affairs. He served honorably as a Trustee on the Board at Texas Tech and ran for Governor of Texas in the Democratic Party primary of 1956.

The Longhorn, too, was picturesque, but his descendants on the range, and in the feedlot, weigh twice as much, make a better feeder and produce more high-priced meat. The open, trackless range was mysterious and romantic, but the wire fence saves money for ranchers, cuts down on the losses in strays and winter storms, and allows a much better use of the land.

Like the "blanket Indian," the stage coach, the buffalo and other institutions associated with the pioneer era, the cowboy has given way to the irresistable forces of civilization. We may regret his passing, but in the final analysis the evolution has been for the best and the West is the gainer. The world moves on, but leaves us the memory of the past to enjoy and profit by.

There has always been a lot of romantic nonsense about the old-time cowboys, most of which has been created by writers for movies and television who probably got their basic plots and character studies from the pulp magazines and dime novels devoted to volume sales and read by the tender hearts in eastern big cities. In reality, the cowboy was a down-to-earth, uncomplicated, far from romantic figure.

After mingling with working cowboys and real old-timers for more than a half-century, Evetts bears witness to the fact that there were only a few whose education extended beyond the most rudimentary lines. Here and there he ran across a puncher who claimed and sometimes, like himself, proved a college education. In nearly every instance these educated men were far more wild and woolly and disreputable in their conduct than the most illiterate western-raised boy that ever turned a cow. Invariably they were renegades of the worst sort who drank, gambled, caroused and indulged to the limit in excesses of every kind.

Many of the best wagon bosses were Texas-born men who could neither read nor write. But they knew cows to the very last degree, would ride any horse that could be saddled and could handle a round-up outfit of twenty-five or thirty men with ease. I have been told, and Evetts will back me up, that top wagon bosses were absolutely without fear of man or beast, fighting fools of the first water. It has been told of trail herds from the Pecos country in Western Texas coming through Eastern New Mexico with ten or fifteen men with the wagon, eighty percent of whom could endorse their name on the back of a check only with the utmost difficulty and a heavy strain on their mentality. But they were just about the average of the men of the plains of those days. Sober, they were peaceable and careful of their actions. Drunk, they were brainless fools looking eagerly for trouble and usually finding it. Theirs was a wild, free life. When they drifted into town after two or three months' absence on the round-up and filled up with red licker, they desired to shoot up the town and otherwise enjoy themselves, and objected strenuously to interference by the city marshal or the sheriff.

Few of the early cowboys had but a hazy idea of the value of money, except that with it they could purchase drinks, fancy silk handkerchiefs, high-heeled boots, Stetson hats with twenty-dollar "rolls" on them, pearl-handled six-shooters and oceans of cartridges with which to pepper signal targets along the railroad on the way out of town or to devastate the glass insulators on the telephone and telegraph poles. They were hospitable to the traveler or visitor to their camps, but so was everyone in those days. Visitors were not so common and a newcomer dropping in to spend the night was twice welcome for he brought the gossip from town or the last cow camp at which he had "hung up." And there were other ways of welcoming visitors devised by the cowboys that were not always as gentle or calm as one might expect. Cowboys liked their fun, too, and especially when it came at the expense of a dude.

Mary Whatley Clarke told an interesting story about the reception given a certain "dude" who visited a cow camp in search of a perfectly hand-tooled chuck wagon, done in miniature by the cowboys of the JA Ranch. This story, which appeared in *The Cattleman*, "was told by J. Evetts Haley, past president of the Panhandle-Plains Historical Society, and a member of the board of directors and executive committee, who dropped in one rainy morning for a cup of coffee. Haley was the first hired field director of the Panhandle Plains Museum. At that time, 1928, the Society held its meetings in the basement of the Administration Building of West Texas State Teachers College at Canyon, where its meager exhibits were housed.

"Haley, a native son of the High Plains, well known writer and natural born cowboy, was then working for the Society, and spent his time hustling exhibits. He had heard about the miniature chuck wagon on the JA Ranch, made by Clinton Henry, manager, and Jimmie Moore, cook. It has been used as a centerpiece for the Christmas table at the annual holiday party.

"Haley coveted the wagon for the new museum. So did other field representatives from other museums. He rode out to the JA one spring day during round-up time and asked to spend his vacation there. Henry told him that they did not run a dude ranch and had no time for city slickers. Haley replied, 'If you will give me an old gentle horse I'll help with the round-up.'

"The cowboys looked at him with bemused and jaundiced eye, and told him he could ride Widow Maker, (one of the wildest broncos on the big spread.) To their surprise the lean college boy stayed on, and later when he showed real skill at 'californianing' a calf, the seasoned cow punchers stopped their pranks. Before Haley left they had given him the little chuck wagon, including a hand-carved miniature horse, tiny pots and pans, etcetera. It is valued at $10,000. Today it is a must for all visitors. It is so meticulously made that the wheels can be removed and the axles greased."

Times changed. The "hell-for-leather" cowboy disappeared and with him those other picturesque characters who spawned an enduring image. But although times have changed and the Old West has disappeared, the spirit of those days lives on, chronicled for us in song, in drama, in fiction, and in historical writing. From the pen of Evetts Haley has come some of the finest history of the Old West, writing which entertains, yet which nourishes the intellect and the imagination.

Ride with Evetts along the trail of years. You'll soon discern the strong personality, ready wit, keen humor, penetrating insight and salty language that have made him a man to be admired and a friend to be treasured.

Reared on the semi-arid plains of West Texas, in a land where gramma grass seemingly stretches without limit to meet a cloudless sky, educated in colleges symbolized by the buffalo and the longhorn, employed by these same institutions to collect specimens of a vanishing era, hired by others to oversee their ranches or riding his own range — these furnished the background for much of the detailed research which has gone into his writing.

From the record we know that J. Evetts Haley was born in the quiet, central Texas farming community of Belton on July 5, 1901. His parents endowed him by natural descent with the gentlemanly traits of a Southerner and an indomitable pioneering spirit. One grandfather, Dr. James Haley, was a Mississippi planter before migrating to Texas following the War Between the States, and the other, William Caperton "Brazos Bill" Evetts, had been a Texas trail driver. Both men saw service in the Army of the Confederacy. His great-grandfather, James Evetts, was a veteran of the Texas Revolution and fought with Sam Houston in the Battle of San Jacinto. It is difficult to imagine a heritage more fitting to a Texan.

After a brief period of ranching in Sterling County, the Haley family moved, by way of Roscoe, to Midland, in 1906. It was there that Evetts matured.

Upon receiving his Master of Arts Degree in History from the University of Texas in 1926, he began a life-long love affair with his chosen subject. He was now officially an historian. His mission, as defined by Homer Carey Hockett, "to transmit knowledge of the past. History is a nation's memory, perpetuating its deeds, its aspirations and ideals. It makes the past a part of us, shapes our deeds in many ways, and links past and present with the future, making all one."

To Evetts, history has most often taken the form of collective biography. His approach is predicated upon the belief that men make history and his carefully selected subjects have been rugged western characters filled with valor, vision, vitality or some other equally redeeming quality. Consider these remarkable personalities, each the subject of a Haley historical biography, men who stood head and shoulders above the common herd: Charles Goodnight, Jeff Milton, Charles Schreiner, John Armstrong, Bob Beverly, John Baylor, Earl Vandale, George Littlefield, Erle Halliburton, James D. Hamlin, Jim East, Quanah Parker and Ranald Mackenzie.

These fearless and energetic men were endowed with voracious appetites for adventure. Innate in their beings was the will to triumph, even against overwhelming odds, or when the struggle seemed hopeless to everyone but themselves. Each man emerged wiser in the laws of nature and of nature's God — a knowledge which fired their passionate approach to life. These old-time cowboys were men of character and such were their deeds that J. Evetts Haley, a man of similar persuasion, saddled up and trailed them to their journey's end. Each of his biographies is not only a memorial in print, but is the embodiment of the local color, the mores, the language and the history of West Texas at that time.

If Evetts had written nothing else, his six major historical books would have established his reputation. His first book, *The XIT Ranch of Texas and the Early Days of the Llano Estacado*, is an epic account of the largest and most famous ranching operation of the early West. It is one of the most highly regarded landmarks in the literature of the cattle country. In it we meet Coronado searching for the Seven Cities of Cibola, Josiah Gregg, Indians, Mexicans, outlaws, and Texas cowmen. Here also are met the first stock grazing on native grass, the smell of burning hair from the first XIT brand, and ranchers who built fences and windmills, and finally, the change from longhorn to fat cow and the nesters who plowed, built homes, and reared families.

It is interesting to note that James D. Hamlin, who did more than any other man to further Evett's early career as a writer and historian by hiring him to do *The History of the XIT Ranch* in 1927, was the subject, after a span of 46 years, of one of his more recent books "The Flamboyant Judge."

Fort Concho and the Texas Frontier began as a history of San Angelo and grew to no less than a history of West Texas in its heroic age. It embodies Evetts Haley's unequalled knowledge of the country, and his familiarity with every water hole and spring, the exploration of every trail, and the establishment of every military post, gained from intimate knowledge and personal acquaintance with hundreds of salty characters. The Sons of the Texas Republic gave *Fort Concho* the Summerfield Roberts award as the best book on the frontier history of Texas in 1952.

Two handsome volumes of historical interest are *The Heraldry of the Range, Some Southwestern Brands,* profusely illustrated with lively drawings from brand books and stock directories, and *Some Southwestern Trails.* The latter work chronicles the various trails which cut this area into a variety of patterns. The book grew out of an advertising idea of the Shamrock Oil and Gas Corporation. After Houston Harte of the *San Angelo Standard-Times* and Carl Hertzog saw the articles they got permission to bring them out in book form and the result is a strikingly beautiful volume that memorializes the old but eternally fresh Southwestern trails.

Life on the Texas Range, a volume containing a hundred photographic prints of life and work of the cowboy on the range, by Erwin E. Smith, with text by Evetts Haley was an endeavor which resulted from a concern with the lurid but popular misrepresentation of the cowboy.

Prepared for them on the 25th anniversary of the company, *Story of the Shamrock* is a business history narrating the early beginnings, struggles and hard work of the men of vision who established and guided the Shamrock Oil and Gas Corporation, the breed of men Haley admires and writes about.

Of course there had to be deviations from the accepted pattern, like some of the articles and books dealing with outlaws: *The Comanchero Trade, Horse Thieves,* and one of his most recent books, *Robbing Banks Was My Business, the Story of John Harvey Bailey, America's Most Successful Bank Robber.*

When Evetts got riled up, fought for a cause, or defended his beliefs, then, too, there were more articles and books. These were brought on by the New Deal's dictatorial control of American agriculture and its inane tampering with the free marketplace. There was "Cow Business and Monkey Business" in the *Saturday Evening Post,* "The Cows Are in the Cotton Patch" and "Texas Control of Texas Soil." Powerful broadsides appeared over Haley's name, castigating the growing bureaucracy in Washington. His political writing reaching its peak in *A Texan Looks At Lyndon,* one of the most cussed and discussed books of the century.

During the period 1948 to 1962, Evetts sent out some delightful Christmas greetings, most of which were small books or pamphlets rather than cards. Evetts did the writing and the illustrations were by Harold Bugbee, one of his most intimate life-long friends, who illustrated many of his books and articles. Printing was at first done by George Autry and later by Carl Hertzog. In 1948, for example, he immortalized one of his cows, "Old Maude," and circulated the essay "in a limited edition among my friends just for the hell of it." In this highly entertaining story there is a great deal of humor at the cost of the government; or, as Evetts wrote, "It seems high time to take the bull by the horns and say a good word for the cow."

In "Christmas at the Hancock House" issued in 1953, Evetts depicts the strong-willed Miss Jennie who let her Southern breeding overcome prejudice by nursing a Yankee soldier back to health. The story ends with Miss Jennie's Christmas blessing: "Thank the Lord! Peace on Earth, Good will to all men, even to a Yankee."

For the 1955 production, Evetts sent out a heartwarming message about today's cowboy, who, in contemplation on the open range at Christmas, is warmed by lasting hope and faith, in harmony with Nature's God. The opening paragraph is rythmically poetic: "When the frost has chased the green back to the grass roots, when the golden leaves of the cottonwood have faded into rustling wraiths upon the ground, and when the stars, in eternal faithfulness, bathe the cattle ranges in a cool and ghostly light, scattered men with mounts still keep lonely vigil over herds."

And the story ends on a fitting note in which the spirit of the season is effectively captured. "But Christmas without contemplation is meaningless, and contemplation thrives best in solitude. No solitude has been so productive of spiritural regeneration as that imposed by desert ranges, where Nature's God denied material abundance, but compensates with lasting hope and faith . . . with the benediction of the Spirit — the undeniable heritage of us all."

Additionally, although there were others of note, we must mention the three outstanding, beautifully illustrated small volumes published by Evetts and the Shamrock Oil and Gas Corporation at Christmas 1960 through 1962. These were *F. Reaugh — Man and Artist, Christmas in the Palo Duro,* and *Then Came Christmas for Mildred Taitt.*

J. Evetts Haley has often characterized himself as "A historian by profession and a cowpuncher by preference." As a young boy he wanted to be a cowboy and one of his first jobs was punching cows during vacations on the Long S Ranch, north of Big Spring, for thirty dollars a month, up to the time he graduated from high school. Of this latter event he says: "I got my purple suede diploma that morning, and I had my saddle ready. I went home and told Mama to put the diploma away because that is the last evidence of an education I want to get." However, Mama persuaded him to further develop his natural interest in history at West Texas State College in Canyon. "At Canyon," he recalls, "I buckled down to studying. I thought a man had to work hard if he went to college, and I didn't realize that education was largely the means of passing four frivolous years."

Asked which of his books he thought was his best, he answered that he regards the biography of Charles Goodnight, the result of over ten years of research, as his best work. "The book," Evett says, "is more than the biography of a man — it is the background of my own soil, a part of my own tradition." The book has successfully withstood the test of time.

In a recent issue of *Persimmon Hill*, the incomparable quarterly publication of the National Cowboy Hall of Fame and Western Heritage Center, the question is asked by Editor/Managing Director Dean Krakel, "I wonder how long we will have to wait for a book to appear that is as solid, careful, historically true and as well written as J. Evetts Haley's *Charles Goodnight: Cowman & Plainsman?*"

Mr. Krakel is both critical and pessimistic about the trend of western thought today. "The Old West," he writes, "is rapidly becoming both faceless and nameless. I have an eerie feeling about the future of our western heritage unless westerners get off their rear ends and oppose those who discredit our history or want to change basic and time-honored customs of western life."

J. Evetts Haley's unmatched ability makes him an ideal author to perpetuate the Old West. The movies and television have romanticized and bastardized the land and its people — the men and women who loved it and tamed it. Evetts Haley, on the other hand, has lived and worked in the cattle country; its people are his friends and its ways are his. He understands the drama of the range country intimately, as an observer and as a participant.

Cowman, author, historian, rancher, politician, philosopher — he has written twenty books and countless articles, essays and political tracts. He has slept in a dugout on the Plains, and has crossed the Atlantic by sea and air. He has lectured on art in San Antonio, and generously ventilated a line shack on the barren expanses of far West Texas peppering rats with a .45. He once ran in the primaries as a Democratic Party candidate for governor and years later served as Republican Party chairman of Randall County. He has cooked up countless batches of sourdough biscuits over open fires on many a dusty round-up. He has ridden bucking horses in rodeos and piloted a Mercedes-Benz along dusty roads in the Canadian River breaks of the Texas panhandle. He wrote and published the all-time best seller by a Texas author, with more than 7,000,000 copies in print. As general range manager for J. M. West, he bossed the largest individually owned ranching operations in Texas.

For more than fifty years Evetts has collected western art, literature, documents and memorabilia. The collection is now housed in the Nita Stewart Haley Memorial Library at Mid- land. There are approximately 10,000 volumes, and its worth is inestimable because of the unique nature of its contents. The library files contain the finest collection of personal interviews with pioneers assembled anywhere. In addition, there are old ranch records and countless items of correspondence among the many unique items found nowhere else. The library is un-equalled as a source for historical research.

The existence of the Nita Stewart Haley Memorial Library affords Evetts a rare opportunity. If he would curtail and elim-inate many of his extraneous activities and set his mind to once again recapturing the action and spirit of the Old West, as he has done so well and so often in the past, he could add priceless chapters to the history of a fabulous region, an endeavor for which he is so admirably equipped.

2

A BOOKMAN'S VIEW OF J.E.H.

by Al Lowman

My introduction to the writing of J. Evetts Haley came in 1955, when I chanced to see a copy of *Fort Concho and the Texas Frontier* on a shelf belonging to my teacher and friend, Dr. William C. Pool of San Marcos. I was attracted immediately by the distinctive beauty of the book, the striking pen-and-ink drawings, and the promise of rousing subject matter. It was an introduction not only to Haley, but to typographer Carl Herzog and illustrator Harold Bugbee. My fascination with their work continues to this day. Their first collaboration was in a 1944 volume about Charles Schreiner of the Texas Hill Country; their last, before Bugbee's death in 1962, was *Christmas in the Palo Duro* issued by the Shamrock Oil and Gas Company.

In my own estimation, their greatest venture was *Fort Concho*. In 1958, I bought a copy from Dudley Dobie for twenty dollars; it was more than I could then afford, but that book has given me countless hours of pleasure. The finest talent of three notable West Texans is assembled in perfect register between its covers. Bugbee's special forte was his native High Plains, with its buffalo, longhorn cattle, and mounted men of action. Haley's sweeping prose matches the illimitable terrain, and Hertzog finished the volume with a handsome buckram binding that approximates the reddish-brown hue of Concho River mud. Truly a desert island choice for a book lover.

Haley's prose bespeaks a respect for and mastery of the English language. It rolls in such majestic phrase that if it is not exactly suited for carving in granite, then it might at least be branded in cowhide. One is constantly delighted at his ability to find new ways of expressing timeworn sentiments. Cliches are as scarce in his prose as cockleburs in his pasture. He limns people, places, and events with the deft, sure strokes of the artist that he is. The style never becomes turgid; it is frequently enlivened with characterizations drawn in anecdote. He is, in J. Frank Dobie's verdict, "raconteur par excellence."

As a writer, Haley appears to have been born, like Minerva, in full maturity. His first publication as a professional historian came in *The Dallas Morning News* on June 28, 1925. The twenty-three-year old chronicler paid tribute to the memory of a beloved Panhandle pioneer, "Aunt Hank" Smith of Crosby County, who had died on the fifth of the month. He sketched the details of her life against the broad canvas of High Plains history, demonstrating with his first published work that he understood the necessity of perspective in evaluating historical subjects, a lesson learned no doubt from the estimable Eugene C. Barker, whom Haley admired, emulated, and perhaps imitated during and after his student days at the University of Texas.

He never treats any writing lightly; the literary quality is always present. Three days after the great dust storm of April 14, 1935, Haley sent a dispatch to the farm and ranch editor of the *Dallas News*. Few correspondent dispatches were ever so dramatic as this one. "For many weeks," he began, "the Panhandle people have hardly seen the sun through a dusty sky. At times it cannot be seen at all and ususally when beyond the meridian it may be gazed upon with as much impunity as a full moon. Sometimes it rises above the mists of silt two hours late and fades from view in the cloudless skies just as much too soon."

In a letter to Walter Prescott Webb a half dozen years later, Haley described another facet of Panhandle existence:

"You have probably gathered," he wrote, "that we have been engaged as usual, and as it will be in the future, in a rough tussle with the weather. After that storm in January, I saddled a short-coupled, rock-bottomed horse that could plow like a caterpillar, and headed for the Rocking Ds, the ranch we have some twelve to fourteen miles west. I crossed Lake Creek, upon which we are located, on the ice, and picked the ridges and the high country, through the sandhills to the west, trying to keep out of the deep drifts. When I reached Carson Creek, named for old Kit, the snow was banked across it in gentle riffles. I got to the west side, where sandhills rise high, wind-blown, and steep from the bed of the creek, and tried to make it out. Buster was a-sweating, and his square-built quarters were churning his tight little frame through the belly-deep snow with a powerful stride. The sandhills were almost in reach when he stopped; my tapaderos were setting deep in the snow; Buster made no traction — he had high-centered. We backed out, took a circle, hit the bank at another spot, and soon Buster and I were snaking up the bare, brown ridges that mark the shifty crests of the Carson sandhills for miles in every direction, high, but not dry, and frozen into a fine footing for Buster's confident stride. But we were soon off these, and breaking through the drifts of the choppy little hills beyond, where the tall red sage grass sometimes stuck through the snow; sometimes merely humped up under the snow and ice in miniature hills itself."

A resume of favorite passages from the work of J. Evetts Haley is so extensive a task as to quickly generate frustration. *Charles Schreiner, General Merchandise,* published by the Texas State Historical Association, contains several fine anecdotes. My favorite is about tough old Creed Taylor, survivor of war, drought, pestilence, and feudists' bullets. One day the nonagenarian veteran stalked into the Schreiner store in quest of tobacco. "That's not good for your health, Mr. Taylor," bantered a friendly sales clerk. The reply was a well-aimed put down: "Young man, I don't smoke for my health."

Throughout his long literary career, Haley has sought to preserve the evanescent vision of a pristine range where no white man had left permanent tracks until the appearance of Charles Goodnight, the subject of a magisterial biography — by Haley. In it, the old man recalled, "Most of the time we were solitary adventurers in a great land as fresh as a spring morning, and we were free and full of the zest of darers."

Haley feels this same exhilaration, the same challenge of life in a land that is often reluctant to confer its bounty on those who dwell thereon. Native writers (especially those who grew up west of the ninety-eighth meridian) are fond of pointing out that much of their Texas resembles the biblical lands — a hot, dry, desert country rimmed with bleached blue hills. It is the kind of environment in which religious philosophies are conceived. The very act of living in West Texas seems to be a religious experience for many who call it home, or so it appears to those of us who live in slightly better-watered climes. In a 1952 Christmas greeting, Haley gave eloquent expression to this outlook.

"Of necessity we live by faith," he wrote, "not in rebellion against but in conformity with Nature's laws. In Her infinite wisdom nothing is slighted and nothing lost. What we are denied in substance we are compensated in hope and expectation. The materialistic world, unable to feel, cannot be expected to understand. It may rebel but it will not remain. Therefore it seems to us that Christmas on these western Plains — though forbiddingly cold and usually severe — glows with an inner, brighter, more kindly light. For this, our chosen if not our promised land, awes us into humility with its cataclysmic violence, toughens our natures to eternal perseverance by its rugged discipline, and turns our hearts to reverence as the only real refuge from her physical storms.

"Hence for us, with deeper poignancy and vaster spiritual import, was it originally written: 'Faith is the substance of things hoped for, the evidence of things not seen.'

"And so it must be on the ranges of grass."

J. Evetts Haley has spent his life — that part out of the saddle — staking down the claim of West Texas and its denizens to a proper place in the annals of history. He has done it with dedication and effectiveness and, in the process, has made himself no less a legend than certain of the figures he has enshrined in his monumental biographies. In fierce old age Charles Goodnight once declaimed, "I'll be damned if I could ever find time to lie in the shade!"

Judging from the extent of this bibliography, neither can Haley.

3

THE CARE AND KEEPING OF MEMORY: J. EVETTS HALEY AND PLUTARCHIAN BIOGRAPHY

by Dr. Melvin E. Bradford

There are a great many sides to the career of J. Evetts Haley, each of them equally colorful. And it *is* difficult to sort them out. For the rancher has sometimes obscured the public man and the public man the scholar. Yet I believe that there is a key to all the activities of this remarkably vigorous and exceptional personage and that this key is made visible in one facet of his intellectual life, in his penchant for celebrating, through the medium of Plutarchian biography, the manner of men who formed and gave a character to his West Texas homeland. Early in his life Haley acquired the discipline of the social scientist and had a promising career as an academic historian: that is, until his political integrity cost him all such prospects.[1] Moreover, he has been one of the great collectors of Texas and Southwestern historical materials.[2] But the essential character of his mind and spirit and the thrust behind his total career are nowhere else made so visible as in the frontier *heldenleben* which have flowed from his pen. These works are, on the one hand, thorough and straightforward biographies of members of "the old breed." They are also something else again — generically the only formal equivalent of the epic now possible in our largely skeptical and deracinated world.

Now, if we recall something of the epic before it lost its essentially heroic character and was transformed into a vehicle for explorations of teleology, it becomes easy to understand why the Plutarchian biography can for our time stand in place of the high heroic poem.[3] For as biography it may keep the appearance of disinterested concern for the "facts" of history and the mysteries of "personality" — two great modern preoccupations. Yet Plutarchian biography has by definition a unity of action and an overarching social and ethical emphasis.[4] It intends with narrative to move the will as well as to inform the reason, to excite enthusiasm or hostility at certain bygone examples of conduct. It presupposes a reasonably homogeneous audience ready to attend a "speaking picture." And it likewise presupposes (with all poetry) that a progression of images or narrative is more useful in moving or informing men than is a mere philosophical argument. Hence the ethical burden, in the best of these works, is not too obtrusive. Their rendering of conduct under pressure is expected, through verisimilitude and dramatic vividness, to earn the right to admonish an audience. Tone is also involved in this effect, and the use of telling episodes or portraits from life. Likewise dialogue. The points of tangency with the epic as form are thus obvious — as is the epic-like use of a past heroic age of a particular people to reproach their decadent present. Paul Fussell calls the purchase of such art on the unsuspecting reader "elegiac action."[5] And such is assuredly what Haley's biographies intend to produce.

The first of Haley's biographies is probably the most important. *Charles Goodnight, Cowman and Plainsman* is a central document in the literature of the Southwest — as much a work of art as it is a study of a man and a culture.[6] Like most of these narratives, it is grounded upon a personal acquaintance and affinity with its subject. Its response is to a whole man, and particularly to the verve and exuberance, honor and courage with which he performed in creating a world. Here, of course, is another epic analogy. For Haley's chosen exemplars are either founders or models of their frontier milieu. They make or sustain something, sum it up in themselves. And of Colonel Goodnight, as he turned westward from the settlements to open the trail to New Mexico and Colorado, Haley was able to write "that he traced his name as well as his trail across the face of the Western World . . . [from which] rose the tradition of the man" (127). The life of Goodnight is punctuated by telling bits of dialogue and quotations from the frontiersman's own memoirs or the recollections of his friends. Its central narrative is framed by the appropriate cast of supporting characters and worthy enemies, and by their lesser adventures.[7] Moreover, the dark and inexplicable forces of nature are allowed a more than insignificant role. But Goodnight stands at the center, with friends and followers and even the setting as a cast.

The first major section of the biography, beginning shortly after a little genealogy and some recollection of Texas in the mid-nineteenth century, is the tale of Goodnight's youthful years as individual soldier and Indian fighter.[8] It is an appropriate prologue to the middle portion of the biography (and its most heroic component), the Goodnight of the cattle drive.[9] Then, finally, come the years after 1875 and Goodnight the founder; the settled rancher and cattle king; the prince come into his majority and able to build what would endure.[10] Yet the most durable image of Charles Goodnight left to us by Haley's book is that of the old man remembering, a Goodnight whom Haley knew in his own person. Here is visible the oracle, here the image of the last test passed with spirit, recapitulating a whole way of life. Harold Nicolson has written that *Beowulf* was the first of the English biographies.[11] And whether or not this is true, J. Evetts Haley's *Charles Goodnight, Cowman and Plainsman* certainly owes something to that poem's pattern, moving as it does through the sequence just described, and concluding as it does with the image of the faithful retainers, in the place of mourning, with the words of reverence on their lips.[12]

Like his life of Goodnight, Haley's other Plutarchian biographies make full use of their hieratic moments and build
toward an elegiac conclusion which their narrative substance
makes to seem inevitable. This is as true of *George W. Littlefield, Texan* as it was of its predecessor.[13] But the Major's
memorial was not carved on his Austin headstone or established with the West Texas town that bears his name. Neither
was it in his ranches or his bank. Haley concludes this work
with Littlefield as benefactor and protector of the University of
Texas: of the university, as he understood it, "in primary
allegiance to the soil that supported it . . . representative of the
history and traditions, the life and attitudes, the ways and
customs — in a word, the culture — of its own land."[14] Hence
Haley's subtitle. For Littlefield's monument as one kind of
Southerner was a portion of the history of his states's principal
university and remains visible in his bequests to the school. He
was no defeatist, but one of those "vigorous men impelled by
strong wills and sustained convictions to carry their aspirations, ideals, and convictions to positive ends" who made
Texas, after 1865, something a little different from its sister
states to the east.[15] And how he used the fortune which he
made in building Texas — in attempting to perpetuate his kind
— is an extension of that will and those seemingly private ends.
Littlefield's assistance to kindred and friends, his interest in
education and the production of a native leadership, was evident as soon as the Major returned from distinguished service
in the Army of the Tennessee and a terrible wound at Mossy
Creek (207-281). For George Littlefield never changed, never
forgot, and never looked back. Despite his roots in plantation
Texas, he, like Goodnight, got on his feet on the cattle trail
north (49-80). And once again like Goodnight, he founded,
after droving, a great ranch. Littlefield's ventures into banking
and politics and his Austin establishment bespeak the civility of
his origins. "A businessman first, a cowman next," he was not
quite the frontiersman.[17] But he and the "lord of the Panhandle" were more alike than they were different. Either one
could "kill his man" when necessary.[18] Either one could be gen-
erous to a fault. They were, in their later days, both patriarchs
and commanded absolute loyalty among hosts of men. And
both fought the new dispensation, when it came on, with word

and deed. Indeed, it is finally surprising how much their lives overlap — that is, until we remember who it is who has chosen to recall them in print.

On first appearance, Haley's other full-scale biography seems to differ considerably from its predecessors. But only on first appearance! *Jeff Milton: A Good Man with a Gun* concerns not a founder but a protector.[19] What this son of Florida's Confederate governor protected, however, links him inextricably with the two great cattlemen of the earlier books. For Jeff Milton kept the law which made possible the major work of a Goodnight or a Littlefield. From Texas to Arizona, from Ranger days to Wells Fargo service to border patrolling in his old age, Milton faced down the worst and the best: or rather, the best at doing the worst. Haley's subtitle is the same sort of double-entendre: Milton was a fine man, an indestructible embodiment of the elder Southern chivalry, who was also good at his work, good with a gun. There is no separating his character from his tools as he himself specified in saying that he would be ready to die only "when I get too old to pull a trigger and lay a man down."[20] For Milton never separated his nature from his function, "never killed a man who didn't need killing" or "shot an animal except for meat."[21] And to this, in the oracular postlude to his career, he added "if a man needs killing, either kill him or be a cur."[22]

In some respects *Jeff Milton: A Good Man with a Gun* is Haley's most complete book. Its record of incidents is exhaustive. A little ranching is included, a little prospecting and certain other enterprises. But the core of the book is a sequence of exploits and encounters whose effect is accumulative.[23] For Milton covered the Southwest in the years when it was settled. In one sense, he was instrumental in that development: and his life, in chronological sequence, is a miniature of its process. The famous Black Jack's Band and the terrible John Wesley Hardin were routine business to Milton in his prime.[24] In the course of his 85 years he came to know a great cross-section of the region: cattlemen, politicians, outlaws, Mexicans, prospectors, and simple settlers. In their midst, alone or in company, a Southerner with a high heart, a passion for friendship, adventure and a devotion to honorable work had a chance to live at the top of his bent, to emulate the William Wallace of

45

his boyhood dreaming. Haley's conclusion to this biography deserves quotation in full. For it completes the construction which precedes it:

> The call of honor and high adventure carried him through a vivid and colorful career that has few equals for fantastic deed and peerless daring in all our history. In the lush woods of Florida, on the Staked Plains of Texas, in the cool crags of the Rockies, and on the shimmering sands of the desert, Jeff Davis Milton was simply Sir William Wallace on a cow horse.
>
> The hostile growth of the Arizona desert, resisting drought and death with seemingly indomitable fortitude, had cast its lacy and lovely shade for him for sixty years. And when his tempestuous life gave way to death, his frail widow carried his ashes back to where the stark suppliant dignity to the God of the bright and eternal skies . . .
>
> So long as free people burnish the bright badge of courage, cherish the traditions of genuine chivalry, and revere the memory of honorable men, so long they should not forget him.[25]

The remainder of Evetts Haley's biographical work is on a smaller scale — the brief *Charles Schreiner, General Merchandise: The Story of a Country Store*, the composite portraits of ranch folk in *The XIT Ranch of Texas and the Early Days of the Llano Estacado* and of soldiers in *Fort Concho and the Texas Frontier*, plus a number of sketches and introductions, many of them gathered in the pamphlet, *Men of Fiber*.[26]

The Schreiner book is the history of an enterprise more than the record of a man and his family. It is assuredly related to Haley's *heldenleben*. And the reader is left with no doubt of the value of a good general store to a frontier community like Kerrville, of a store that fits the people it serves so well that it becomes "an ideal and a tradition."[27] But Captain Charles, despite Haley's clear admiration for his extremely useful life, and despite certain difficult moments in his career, cannot quite reach the heroic measure. Storekeeping of his kind makes for stability, continuity and "typical Texas." Yet the end result is, at best, social and economic exemplum, a humane and culturally responsible concentration on that usefulness and its rewards. Said another way, the shadow of death does not hang over his deeds; the exultation that goes with being under that shadow does not animate their performance. Haley's first book, the study of the XIT, contains in its vignettes and its reflections on cowboy life what the Schreiner book lacks, an air of danger, of momentary strain or potential explosion. However, a grim Saxon humor balances and sustains the purchase of these brief intensities.[28] And the effect of the total book is adjunctive to that of Haley's heroic and Plutarchian works. The same holds true of *Fort Concho and the Texas Frontier*, though there the variety of human types observed is greater, the action more complete. I will not tarry to consider merits in these books that are beside my point. But a few additional observations on *Men of Fiber* are, before my conclusion, appropriate.

In "Biographer's Confession," a prologue to this book, Haley makes overt what is implicit in his full scale biographies. He announces, in plain terms, the Plutarchian motive, even though the five sketches of Men of Fiber are too brief to achieve the requisite effect. Baylor, Parker, Mackenzie, Potter and Beverly are all obviously heroic figures. Action under pressure, performed with grace, defined their lives. And Haley has told a bit of their stories for a reason: because they are his "own people," are in effect "blood-brothers"; and because they "have a place in the minds of healthy children" and "deserve a niche in the mellow memories associated with age."[29] For they "looked resolutely into the setting sun" and faltered not along the trace. From each he gives us a little characteristic speech. From each a few adventures. True, the full power of Plutarchian narrative is not there. For Haley cannot in the compass he allows for himself develop complete scenes or infer a total sensibility. The power of the epic hero is, we remember, derived from what he does — from "what" and "how," without excessive inquiry into "why." But the biographer himself makes up for these lacks and for the absence of a reacting cast of surrounding characters with the assertion of his own response. Nowhere is Haley more plainspoken in announcement of a theory of biographical ends. And nowhere is the link between his composings and the epic-making impulse made more unmistakable.

There are in the total Haley bibliography a great many more brief sketches like those collected in *Men of Fiber*. Those interested in a more inclusive impression of Haley's biographical labors may consult Chandler A. Robinson's careful listing. In addition there are also other related materials in the pieces of occasional lore on the Southwestern scene which Haley continues to bring forth, other proprietary keepings of a prescriptive memory.[30] For the flavor of all of this material is heroic, and the impulse behind it generally epic. And this is to say nothing of the implications of Haley's editing or of the inverted Plutarchianism of *A Texan Looks At Lyndon, A Study In Illegitimate Power*.[31] The flow of Haley's testimony in behalf of his pieties continues unchecked, his posture towards this later day unchanged. Like all heroic poets, he is an anachronism on principle, for reasons announced in the unity and vigor of his art. Thus he belongs to a small company of Texas or Southwestern writers whose temper still bespeaks the "manly" and intrepid origins of their region, even though the age which they honor is "gone forever without leaving anything equally good to replace it."[32]

FOOTNOTES

[1] A brief biographical sketch appears in Chandler A. Robinson's *J. Evetts Haley: Cowman-Historian* (El Paso: Carl Hertzog, 1967), pp. 1-32.

[2] I refer specifically to Haley's collecting of frontier materials for the University of Texas and then for the Panhandle Plains Historical Association.

[3] I assume here the theory of epic which traces the evolution of the genre from unformed cosmological and heroic epic proper (*Beowulf, The Song of Roland*) and from thence to the literary epic (a poem with a hero *and* a teleology) and finally to the *via* (*The Divine Comedy, Paradise Lost, Pilgrim's Progress* and related works principally interested in pointing the way to a better life beyond death).

[4] See R. H. Barrow's *Plutarch and His Times* (Bloomington: Indiana University Press, 1969) and Edgar Johnston's *One Mighty Torrent: The Drama of Biography* (New York: Macmillan, 1955).

[5] *The Rhetorical World of Augustan Humanism* (Oxford: The Clarendon Press, 1965), pp. 283-305.

[6] *Charles Goodnight, Cowman and Plainsman* (Norman: University of Oklahoma, 1949). Many of my page citations to this work and to sequels are within the text.

[7] The chief of these supporting characters are Goodnight's companions in Indian wars, on the cattle trail and in ranching. I would, from their company, single out Oliver Loving and John Chisum.

[8] *Charles Goodnight*, pp. 15-120.

[9] *Ibid.*, pp. 121-275.

[10] *Ibid.*, pp. 276-401.

[11] *The Development of English Biography* (New York: Harcourt, Brace, and Co., 1928).

[12] *Charles Goodnight*, pp. 264-266. This biography is also like *Beowulf* in making its concluding note of tribute seem inevitable by moving through youth, private adventures (section I) to adventures with a small band of retainers and the life of a community at stake (section II) to a final image of the old hero at bay, representing in his own person the character of a whole people (section III).

[13] *George W. Littlefield, Texan* (Norman: University of Oklahoma Press, 1943).

[14]*Ibid.*, p. 270.

[15]*Ibid.*, p. vii.

[16]Actually two great ranches, the LIT and then the LFO (*ibid.*, pp. 80-187).

[17]*Ibid.*, p. 62.

[18]See *Charles Goodnight*, p. 154 and *George W. Littlefield*, p. 53.

[19]*Jeff Milton: A Good Man with a Gun* (Norman: University of Oklahoma Press, 1949).

[20]*Ibid.*, p. 415.

[21]*Ibid.*, p. 411.

[22]*Ibid.*, p. 408.

[23]Here Haley's mastery of quiet understatement and straightforward narrative becomes apparent. The effect, apart from a few courtly passages, is like that of the Old Norse sagas.

[24]*Jeff Milton*, p. 228 and pp. 264-279.

[25]*Ibid.*, pp. 415-415.

[26]*Charles Schreiner, General Merchandise: The Story of a Country Store* (Austin: Texas State Historical Association, 1944); *The XIT Ranch of Texas and the Early Days of the Llano Estacada* (Norman: University of Oklahoma Press, 1967); *Fort Concho and the Texas Frontier* (San Angelo, Texas: San Angelo Standard-Times, 1952); *Men of Fiber* (El Paso: Carl Hertzog, 1963).

[27]*Charles Schreiner*, p. ix.

[28]One of Haley's links to the older heroic materials is his skillful use of ironic understatement in small bits of dramaturgy, especially in treating of grim moments and dangerous men.

[29]*Men of Fiber*, p. 3.

[30]The epic poet, by definition, speaks not for himself but for a whole people. And he speaks to them out of a selective memory of their past, choosing persons and events which may prepare the young to act their part when comes the time of trial. Haley openly addresses much of his work to his own kind and for kindred purposes. Some of his unmentioned sketches salute other memory keepers. Others flesh out his readers' understanding of the circumstances in which his heroes performed.

[31]*A Texan Looks at Lyndon, A Study in Illegitimate Power* (Canyon, Texas: Palo Duro Press, 1964). Haley's total career as biographer prepared him to write this philippic.

[32]"Personal Reflections on Judge Hamlin," p. xxiii of *The Flamboyant Judge: James D. Hamlin*, as told to J. Evetts Haley and William Curry Holden (Canyon, Texas: Palo Duro Press, 1972).

4

A SALTY TEXAS REBEL

by Dave Shanks

On February 25, 1959, the U.S. Supreme Court plowed no new legal ground but did emphasize in a decision the fine line of legal reasoning that now justifies a thick set of federal farm controls, all based on the "commerce clause" of the Constitution.

The court ruled that J. Evetts Haley Jr., of Canyon, Texas, had to pay $406.11 for overplanting by 40 acres a wheat allotment, although he planned to use the wheat to feed his own cattle on his own farm. Interest in the case was heightened by the U.S. Agriculture Department's levy of penalties on a Michigan farmer, Stanley Yankus, who planted wheat to feed his own chickens. Yankus said he might even move to Australia to do his farming.

One of the principals was J. Evetts Haley Sr., who long has been a critic of federal controls, a stormy petrel in Texas politics since the very beginning of the New Deal. Significantly, the Haleys have never participated in any of the farm pro-

grams, have declined nearly $100,000 in subsidy payments in a decade.

James Evetts Haley Sr. is 58. His age is hard to measure, for his kind are men by the time they are 20, and except for a thickening gray in their hair, they change but little after that. He is of medium height, built spare and wiry. He walks with the uncertainty of those men used to heeled boots jabbed through stirrups, uncomfortable when they are ground-tied. He is ruggedly handsome, though his face is sun-gnarled and squinted. He has the leathery complexion of the breed who spend their lives in the abrasive winds and sun and alkali — all signs of drought country — and infrequent floods that brand the Llano Estacado and its subregions in western Texas.

This Estacado is a giant empire of space, tilting some toward the sun from the Canadian River, on the north, and breaking into gentle land waves toward the Concho Rivers on the south. In its unsettled parts, wrote Haley, "a man from the region of landmarks turns into a derelict upon the ocean of grass." This great land of drought and space could inspire the people who lived on it. "The illimitable bounds of these Plains suggest nothing short of infinity, and in the sober reflection imposed by their ringing silences, they threw the isolated traveler back upon himself in contemplation of the spiritual end of man."

At the turn of the century, and before, the Staked Plains tolerated no derelicts. Some may have come who did not fit, either there or where they came from. Those who stayed belonged. And they belonged because they bested the weather and the land, a task still not easy if a man relies on the surface of the earth for his living and has no resources to the hydrocarbons stored toward its middle. Even its under-earth resources are hard to get at, testing in full measure those who try to gain them in underground pockets deeper than almost any in the world.

This is a violent, turbulent country.

To this country, J. Evetts Haley belongs.

He is the region's spokesman whose views are as turbulent as its weather, even disturbing to its conscience. He has traced with knowledge and affection its history. He has written about its people as though they were heroes instead of the social

52

misfits that other historians said they were. He has gathered its "ana" for storage and display in half a dozen collections. It is not by chance that the heritage of this country, bounded by the periphery of the Plains, rubbed off on Haley.

For just over a quarter century, Haley also has been the region's Thomas Paine, a brilliant historian and a provocative political pamphleteer. In his files, kept in a study lined with books of history, folklore and geology of the West, Haley has hundreds of items clearly in the category of political propaganda tracts. In each, he argues implacably that Americans stand to lose their individual liberties to big government, and he insists that they should rely on themselves instead of government for their own welfare. Singularly, Haley has stood with the minority almost since he first became actively interested in politics. But this has not deterred the force of his own expression one whit.

What distinguishes Haley from those others who ostensibly have similar views is his own willingness and determination to live strictly by his code. Sometimes this has had Spartan-like consequences.

. . . He has been pummeled in debate on the courthouse lawn in Amarillo before thousands who had come to hear Homer Price Rainey, a former president of the University of Texas, then a gubernatorial candidate.

. . . In the last decade, he has spurned nearly $100,000 in federal farm subsidies at a time the U.S. Agriculture Department was pouring out more than $20 billion to other farmers and ranchers.

. . . More recently, he has tried, unsuccessfully, to peck a hole in the reasoning of the U.S. Supreme Court, which he says imposes constitutional strictures on individuals, threatening to make government the master of the people.

Why doesn't Evetts Haley quit this personal campaign?

Or, at least, why won't he soften his views and move into the intellectual arena of the new century?

These are the questions asked about Haley.

There probably is but one answer.

Evetts Haley doesn't know how to quit.

"We had so little out there in the Plains. We were always wanting and never realizing," he said. "I was raised in the shadow of the Guadalupe Mountains to the West and the Davis Mountains to the southwest. They were a long, long way off. I was just a kid, but I made up my mnd that one day I would see those mountains. I was a man before I went. But I went."

Haley was born in 1901, in Bell County, a region that by legend had attributes of an uncommon interest in politics almost from the time settlement began. On his mother's side, the Evetts family were old settlers, coming to Texas in 1834. His great-grandfather, Jim Evetts, fought with Sam Houston at San Jacinto. His grandfather, "Brazos Bill" Evetts, so named because of the numerous other Bills in the family, moved up the Brazos River, stopping at old Nashville and Port Sullivan, both just above Bryan, on his way to Bell County. His mother was Julia Evetts, the eldest of 16 children.

The Haley family had come to Texas from Mississippi, a part of that horde of displaced persons who moved into the state after the Civil War. Haley's father had a "speculative turn." He moved his family from the humid areas in Central Texas to the arid west. He ranched in Sterling County, then moved to the Midland country. He retreated eastward, but only briefly, operating a stock farm at Miles, in Tom Green County. By 1910, the Haleys had moved back to the Midland country, and they have headquartered there ever since.

Haley recalls that his mother was the stabilizer for the family. "When the going got rough and tough, dad would worry. Not mother. She was the stoical sort, though she was thoroughly feminine." His mother was a cheerful woman who loved the adventure of the West and the land and seemed not to mind the frontier hardship. "She would say, 'It will always rain — in time.' That has come to have a double connotation in late years," laughs Haley, who, like all cowmen, fears drought worse than any other catastrophe.

In the sameness of these tremendous Plains, Haley recalls with sentimental tenderness "the pathetic desire of the women folk for some sort of culture, the Wednesday Study Club and that sort of thing."

If the frontier was difficult and hard, the people who lived on it were compensated. The nights were usually beautiful, and the awesome space measured in three dimensions took hold of these people. Julia Haley read to her five children on the

54

porch of the clapboard shacks on this ranch or that farm for which the father had traded. Lumber had been hauled to Midland on the Texas and Pacific Railroad, and then by teams to the ranches. This was a land of shallow water. Windmills dotted prairies, and Midland became known as the Windmill City. This water was badly gypped, never very palatable to humans. Fresh vegetables in the indifferent gardens consisted almost altogether of blackeyed peas and squash.

Eventually the Haleys came to live in the City of Midland. His father acquired an interest in the Midland Hardware Company, a firm still existing, and a small ranch near town. Later, the Haleys began buying land in Winkler and Loving Counties, a part of the old W Ranches, near the Texas-New Mexico border, an area where 60 acres are needed to keep one cow. This ranch was 20 miles northeast of Pyote, a full 80 miles from Midland. It was to become the Home Ranches, now operated by Haley's brother, John Haley.

As a kid in the ranch country, Haley worked hard. He once rode Keno, a gray pony, from Midland to the Home Ranch, a two-day trip, to work cattle with the help of only an old cowhand from the W Ranch. On this trip, he scratched his first bed bugs. "As Roy Bedicheck says, 'It ain't what they ate, it's what they beat down that counts.' "

There were no roads, and Haley had to orient his course by the railroad, heading westward from Midland. He stopped at a section house near Duro to spend the night. Finding only old flour, lard, baking powder and syrup, he baked bread for his supper. Self-reliance was something of a necessity in this empty country, for neighbors were few and water was short. Its necessities occurred in many ways, and even simple decisions were urgent and important. "I wanted to turn my horse loose for the night. There was an old burro in the section-sized trap, but I didn't know if it had ever been ridden. I decided to try him out; so, I threw him in the corral and turned out my horse." Haley learned the next morning the burro hadn't been ridden, but he did succeed in catching up his pony. If he had failed, there would have been interminable miles afoot in this grass wilderness.

Like all kids in the ranch country, Haley wanted to be a cowpuncher. During a Christmas vacaton when he was in high school, he worked for Bryant and Elkins, who had leased from C. C. Slaughter the Long S Ranch just north of Big Spring. He liked the job and planned to go back when he graduated from the high school in the spring. "I got my purple suede diploma that morning, and I already had my saddle and gear ready. I went home that noon and told mama to put that diploma away. 'This is the last evidence of education I want to get.' "

Legs Curry ran the Long-S for Bryant and Elkins, and he put his new hand to work with the wagon. One of the cowboys was Jess Slaughter, now Howard County Sheriff. Then Haley was told to ride to Rattlesnake Pasture, a treacherous stretch of country with badger holes covered with long grass. "I was riding Headlight, and we ran into one of those holes. The horse went down like a shot, and I caught my right knee. Somehow, I managed to crawl over to him and ride on into headquarters."

While he was laid up, Haley's mother persuaded him to enroll in the small college at Midland. A year of drought and depression forced the college to close, but his mother insisted that he complete the term at West Texas State College in Canyon, in the Upper Panhandle.

"I got off the train without an overcoat or a trunk. I had a little bit of money, but not enough; so, I turned to carpentering and yard work. I dug a thousand post holes to get by."

History fascinated Haley even then. He already published an essay in *The Midland Reporter* while he was still in high school, and he had renewed his interest in history during the short time he had attended the college in Midland.

"At Canyon, I buckled down to studying. I thought a man had to work hard if he went to college, and I didn't realze that education was largely the means of passing four frivolous years and that a degree had about as much distinction for man as dew-claws has for a cow."

Haley enrolled in courses under Ann I. Hibbetts, a psychologist and an Irish native, and Mary E. Hudspeth, who taught Spanish. He recalls them as stimulating teachers. Strangely, Haley did not encounter economics in any of his courses, though they were heavily weighted in favor of the social sciences. Even now, he says he never has read a formal text on the subject.

"I already knew how to make a living — hard work — what we could raise and produce ourselves was ours."

56

Haley's ideas about economics are elemental, lacking conception of the theoretical framework that marks this complicated discipline now. But, still they are reasonably satisfying to him. An anecdote about the first trunk he had portrays somewhat significantly his ideas of the Acquisitive Society.

"I went home one Christmas from college, and my mother gave me a trunk. She ran a boarding house for some teachers and fed some other people. She was a wonderful cook. She wanted me to have a trunk; so, she decided to do the laundry herself instead of sending it out. She bought this trunk with the money she saved in a till on the side."

This trunk played at least an incidental part — enough for another anecdote — in Haley's historical interests.

"The only theft I ever committed was out in the Sandhills, near Midland. We were going to the ranch, and I saw two of those little flat stones — metate stones — Indians used to grind their grain. I put them in the wagon, planning to take them to the museum in Canyon." Later, Haley put the stones in his trunk to take them back to school. The baggage man threw the trunk off the train, tearing an end out of it. These stones were Haley's first gift to the museum, though by now he has quite a collection there.

Haley earned a degree and went to work for $75 a month for the new Panhandle Plains Historical Society. "Here was a chance for history at home."

Soon afterward, as a graduate student at the University of Texas, Haley encountered one of a handful of intellects that he ever really admired. E. C. Barker, the political historian, probably can claim the distinction of being the only person Haley would willingly defer to, even in the heat of debate. Barker convinced Haley that political history is the most important kind of historical study. "At one time, I thought he was mistaken. Now that I've completed the circle I think he was dead right."

Haley did not complete this intellectual circle until several years later, when, in the 1930s, he came to Austin under a Rockefeller grant to gather historical materials for the University. He happened to read Spengler's *Hour of Decision*. Spengler said, as Haley recalls, "The pursuit of politics is the most important pursuit of man."

With his new degree, Haley was worth $150 a month to the Panhandle Historical Society. He did not take time off for his first fling into journalism as a reporter. Lindsey Nunn and Dave Warren, owner and manager of the *Amarillo News*, sent him to Plainview to report a special hearing of the Texas Railroad Commission. The commission was then settling the routes of the railroads into the Panhandle, principally in the South Plains region. Competing for the routes were Fort Worth and Denver, Santa Fe, Rock Island, and Quanah, Acme and Pacific.

Haley had already begun his historical writings, which are prolific in number and distinguished for their authenticity and literary quality. His first essay was about Old Tascosa, second only to Channing as the oldest town in the Panhandle and 40 miles northwest of Amarillo. He became interested in Charles Goodnight's recollections of the Indians, and later wrote Goodnight's biography, which ranks as a model for that literary form. *The Dallas Morning News* published a feature story about the first windmills and fences in the area. And the *Southwest Review* carried some of his articles.

Haley's first recognition as a historical writer, though, came with publication of his book on the XIT Ranch, a book issued originally as a family memorial for benefit of those related to the owners of the great ranch lying along the Texas-New Mexico line in the Panhandle.

Working for the Panhandle society, Haley also became acquainted with T. D. Hobart, a giant in size and character, a Yankee who managed the J(ohn) A(dair) Ranch near Pampa, one of the largest cow outfits in the Panhandle. The JA owned a diorama depicting a chuck wagon scene. The Panhandle group wanted this diorama for its museum; so did others, particularly an influential group from Ft. Worth.

"I took my saddle and bedroll and went out to the JA," Haley recalls. "I visited some of the hands and did a little cowboying, and the men seemed a little surprised to see a 'man from the college' out there with a saddle."

On one of those unwritten dares, by which a man is expected to prove his mettle with deed instead of jaw, Haley saddled "Magdalina."

"Damned if that horse didn't pitch. But I rode him once, got off for a drink, then took him down in a sandy draw and rode him again." Haley's article on "Cowboys of the JA" appeared in *The Cattleman's Magazine*. A few days later, the JA sent the diorama to Canyon.

The cowboy-historian worked his other professional trails with the same diligence as the Matador and at a hundred other places where the history of the Panhandle country showed through in hidden manuscripts, letters kept in family Bibles, and pieces of ranch gear.

When he was 28, Haley's book on the XIT was published. Aside from his own pride of authorship, which heightened his desire to be a professional among the historians and not just a cowhand on a ranch, publication of the book marked an important point in his career. Until then, a substantial part of his historical work had centered on folklore, the anecdotes to make history interesting but not significant, though some of his research had developed materials importantly new. And until that time, he had been relatively unconcerned with politics, or even its history, except for the classroom insistence of Dr. Barker.

There were expectations, but these were minor. His father and mother were "vigorous partisans, none of this middle-of-the-road stuff for them." He heard their discussions of the issues during his childhood years, and his father was a follower of Joe Bailey and the State's Rights cause. The father was a Democrat, as a Southerner should have been, though he disliked Wilson's internationalism.

In the Panhandle, while he was on the reporting assignment for the Amarillo newspaper, Haley met Frank Kell, a Wichita Falls businessman and an ardent lover of regional history. "He was one of the sharpest men I ever knew. A slender man in his late middle age, Kell was a dominant figure, a student of both history and business." Haley and Kell struck up a friendship that resulted in discussions of various kinds, including politics. (Kell also endeared himself to Haley by purchasing 40 copies of the XIT book.) Haley also was acquainted with J. O. Guelcke of Amarillo, a lawyer remembered by Haley as a "great patriot, a student of politics, and an ardent historian."

In broadest outline, these experiences probably comprised the political interests Haley had had until that time.

The year 1929 was different than most. The nation was plunged into the Great Depression in the fall of that year, increasing the urgency of political discussion everywhere and among all groups. The year had an additional importance to Haley. He had attended a meeting of a folklore society in Austin, and at this meeting he was asked by Dr. Charles Ramsdell if he would come to the University, not to teach but to collect historical materials. Haley did.

During his year of graduate study, he was tremendously impressed by some he had met at the University. The history faculty of that time, he says, was comprised of great minds and men: Barker, the political historian; Ramsdell, the Civil War scholar; Marsh, a witty and profound master of ancient history; Charles W. Hackett, the noted Spanish American authority; E. W. Winkler, the bibliographer; Walter Webb, who had begun to move upward in the scale of historical prestige as an authority on the history of the Great Plains and the Frontier. "Of all the things I ever did . . . To go one year to school there and later to be associated with those men," enthuses Haley.

He set to work on his mission of scholarship with the unscholarly trappings he had had in the Panhandle. Haley threw his saddle over the hood of his car. He recalls that he hauled back to Austin "historical materials by the ton, literally."

"I didn't buy a damned thing like they do now," he comments.

The depression was on, and politics and economics became both unavoidable and inseparable. Not since the Civil War had so many felt the urgency of politics as they did during the campaign and election that swept Franklin Roosevelt into office "on the best platform ever written — but not used — in America."

Almost from the beginning of the New Deal, Haley firmed up his views. They had to encompass economics as well as history. Haley himself dates his bitter hatred of the New Deal from the day Roosevelt abandoned the gold standard. This was April 14, just a few days more than a month after the inauguration on March 4, 1933.

Probably the first time I got unwound," he remembers, "was at a meeting of the Southern Scholarship Societies at the University. Dr. H. Y. Benedict, president of the University, was one of those at the big dinner in the Student Union Building. I had been invited to speak and I had written an address entitled 'Causal Comment on Current Trends.' This later was referred to as 'Caustic Comments'," laughs Haley. This was his first indictment of the New Deal and he says the visiting students were "flabbergasted to hear it criticized."

Haley's debates were confined to the campus. They were salty and vigorous. "Probably the bitterest thing I did involved Bob Montgomery, on the economics faculty." Haley wrote a letter to the Daily Texan, charging that some faculty members in the economics and government departments defended the inflation that was intended to occur by abandoning the gold standard but were gambling in the gold market on the side. "They answered just as salty," adds Haley. "The only persons who agreed with me probably were Caleb Perry Patterson and Dr. Barker, and they agreed just in passing."

Haley was in the President's office one day when Dr. Benedict jokingly asked what he planned to do after the Rockefeller Foundation money ran out.

"I knew I was going to be fired, and I already had sent my wife and baby boy back to Canyon to live. I turned and answered, 'I've punched cows for $40 a month, and I can do it again'."

When Dr. Homer Rainey and the University Regents broke over the traces of academic unanimity over Dos Passos' *U.S.A.* and the dismissal of three economics staff members, Haley recounted with glee the circumstances of his own departure from the Austin campus. This was used in one of his numerous political tracts — "The University of Texas and the Issue." Haley invited J. Frank Dobie "and the other purely academic warriors to come out of the convenient brush of generalities and open up at close range with the cold hard facts."

Dr. Rainey had charged the Regents with violating the principle of academic freedom by firing the instructors. Then to the point of his own dismissal, Haley wrote that an interesting parallel intruded, that he had requested a leave of absence from his job, which he had held for seven years, to write and speak his honest convictions upon a partisan political issue. "He (Haley) was guilty, and he knew it without reading them, of violating the proprieties wrapped up in the 'Rules and Regulations' on academic freedom. He was not fired. He was — in what Dr. Rainey's advocates now charge is euphemistic, dishonest subterfuge — simply 'not reemployed'."

Haley enjoys digging at his adversaries, and he notes that "not a one of these liberals beat his sensitive breast . . . in denunciation of the board for following the rules." This is partial explanation of Haley's version of his dismissal. It is a typical example of his pamphleteering technique. "The sight of a good man eating 5,000 words without any ketchup is not one to comfort the stomach," comments a Haley acquaintance, "and Haley doesn't play by girls' rules. Nobody is immune from his venom, nor does he rattle first." Haley is a partisan, and like his parents, he has no use for middle-of-the-road.

A circumstance of importance interrupted the normal chronology of Haley's career at the University from 1929 to 1936. Earlier, he had foreseen the coming of an inflationary era, though the deflation of this Depression Decade still staggered the nation's economy. Haley bought a ranch of 3,600 acres in the Canadian brakes, just north of Amarillo. His father and brother lived on the Home Ranches, in far West Texas. "I had more to gain by inflation than most people, for inflation would have erased some of our debts."

The New Deal's various programs galled Haley. One especially. The government had begun paying for cattle — condemning those animals declared unfit by inspectors, shipping the rest to relief canneries. His father, J. J. Haley, and brother, John Haley, sent for Evetts, asking him to come to the ranch. "I got there at night. Father and my brother told me they had already notified the government men they were ready to sell their cattle. There was no point discussing the matter." Haley recalls an analogy used during the long argument that followed this announcement: "Cotton the year before; it's just as logical to kill cattle."

Again Haley turned to his typewriter, this time writing for *The Saturday Evening Post*. His article was called "Cow Business and Monkey Business" and in it he described the day they took their cattle to the railroad:

"Range cattle, for the most part, are too poor to throw upon the regular market, and cowmen and farmer have, in the face of conditions partly induced by agricultural monkey business, the option of selling their cattle to the government or letting them starve (because cotton crop controls had raised the price of cottonseed, etc.)

"A few stout-hearted men are following the latter course. But it is a hard one, for of all the heart-rending experiences a cowman has to face, that of helplessly sitting by and watching his cattle starve to death is the worst. We had not the resistance to do so. We joined the movement and sold our dogies and canner cows to the government."

The Haleys hired additional hands and gathered cattle from the far sides of their range.

"Not a spear of green grass tempted a hungry cow, and all day long the whirring of the locusts — the terrible symphony of the drouth — beat in our ears with the bawling of starving cattle. As we broke our first camp and prepared to move on to an adjoining pasture, a neighbor trailed in with his little bunch of cattle on the way to the railroad. Upon their left hips his stock carried the X brand of the government . . ."

"After another day's roundup we were trailing our own herd toward headquarters. When a calf broke back from the drags, we grudgingly eased our horses around him instead of breaking away in the joy of the chase, as we usually do, as sparing of horseflesh as we could be.

"And on that 10-mile drive, little whitefaced calves played out even though we carefully nursed them along while knowing they would be condemned and knocked in the head at the end of the drive. When they stopped from heat and fatigue, we roped and lifted them in the truck that served as a calf wagon, and so hauled them in for inspection.

"Fifty-two cows that were getting old were condemned. The cows huddled pitifully in a fence corner while a .30-.30 rifle knocked one after another to the ground. Cows that had sold for a hundred dollars a head a few years ago were bought by the government at twelve; their condemned calves at four."

Then Haley caustically noted the terms the cowmen paid for these "benefits." The cowmen, he wrote, "agreed to cooperate with (any) further general programs."

Fragments of Haley's narrative point up his concepts of how man and his government ought to exist:

*"The inside of each man's range is inviolate, and before the days of the Brain Trust, no one would have had the temerity to suggest how a cowman should manage his personal affairs.

*"And though our cattle were mortgaged, we managed our business to suit ourselves. Not even the hard-fisted bankers and loan agents . . . ever appended to their notes a blanket agreement by which they might take charge of our affairs.

*"Having seen the development of the range industry under private initiative, we believe the profit system is right and good. But we believe, too, a banker, as a trustee for our and other folks' money, must have collateral; that our notes, executed in good faith, must be met; that unless they are, our banker must and should foreclose.

*"We hold to the simple theory that if we rent 10 horses to a neighbor for a consideration, we should get 10 horses back, no matter what happens to the price of horses and their rate of hire in the meantime.

*"But we have been a simple trusting people, living in an environment where a man had to keep his word or be held to vigorous account. In the meantime, the world has advanced, we are assured, and the homely virtues that we cherished are but outworn dogmas of a selfish age. So far as I know, we are no 'theoretical diehards,' and we never wanted 'special privilege.'

*"Until this day," wrote a disconsolate Haley in 1934, "our people lived without benefit of moratoria and government subsidies."

To the best of his knowledge, this single instance is the only time Evetts Haley had shared in any federal farm program, and even this was not a subsidy, a gift. "They got the cows."

Significantly, Haley and his son, J. Evetts Haley, Jr., encountered government intervention they sought to avoid.

The drouth of the 1950s had been followed by a federal hay program, theoretically aimed at lowering the cost of hay in the drier regions of the Southwest. But Haley decided to hunt for a ranch country with rainfall to beat his part of the drouth hardship.

"Evetts Jr. was doing well with his arguments but was flunking his courses at the University," recounts Haley. "Don't ever believe a government rain report, either. I bought a place on the Lower Arkansas River, in Oklahoma. It had 300 acres in the river bottom. My boy wanted to do some farming. 'I'm a cowpuncher,' I told him, 'but if you want to farm, go ahead'.

"One thing sure, if a man farms, he can get in trouble with the federal government. I bought into a three-year drouth. We planted wheat and we had some pasture." The Haleys harvested a crop and put it in the granary. Evetts Jr. told his father he needed some money: "I'm not going to the bank and borrow any more. Go sell that wheat." Without permission to plant (a certificate), the Haleys couldn't market their wheat.

The Haleys planted another crop and were told they had overplanted by 40 acres. Says young Haley: "When I planted this crop, I had no idea or intention of bucking or testing the allotment. I have never even thought about it. I was thinking only of raising feed for my cattle."

The U.S. Agriculture Department sued the Haleys for $506.11. A Texas district judge, T. Whitfield Davidson, dismissed the suit, declaring: "I can find no constitutional amendment authorizing Congress to tell farmers what to plant, what to eat or how to work."

The Supreme Court found the authorization, relying on a case titled *Wickard vs. Filburn*. The Haleys reasoned that Filburn had taken every subsidy in the book while they had accepted none.

Now, almost on the anniversary month of his breakthrough into politics, Haley indicates 26 years of political fighting, including a strenuous campaign for the governor's job in 1956, was hard. He is a weary campaigner.

"Our only hope is in the little people, those without influence or money. And there are not enough of them. It looks like my boy will either have to quit ranching, take the federal subsidies, or leave the country."

J. Evetts Haley had outlasted the drouth as his mother had told him he could do. He had seen the Guadalupe and Fort Davis Mountains. He had lost in a courtroom.

From *The Austin American-Statesman* Sunday, March 22, 1959, Pp. B-1 - B-2.

5

J. EVETTS HALEY,
MAN AND SCHOLAR

by Savoie Lottinville

I think of him as he was two and thirty years ago, a small man with a large frame of mind, an undeviating courage and strength of conviction, and a twinkling sense of humor on a sun-tanned, small-oval face. When he smiled, he might have been a boy; when he frowned and chose his words with a feeling for their critical value, you knew he was a man — a man who had no patience for soft thinking and questionable dealing. He somehow conformed to the idealized description of a Western cowman. Idealized? Indeed, he was one of a kind. Where in Eugene Manlove Rhodes or Owen Wister or George Pattulo could you find his like? Western men to be sure, but here was also a mind honed sharp by many adventures at the edge of reality, where men of strong character won their way by incredible striving. These he chose for his own: Charles Goodnight, George W. Littlefield, Jeff Milton, and a corporate personality, the XIT Ranch of Texas. His biographies of them, won in painstaking and long extended research, were so written that they had the status of classics the day they respectively appeared. There were others, and at least one of them shook an entire Democracy (the capital letter here is intentional). And he was right.

Being right about oneself is another, sometimes more difficult matter. Vanity and self-seeking often get in the way. The man from the Brakes of the Canadian never sought or cultivated a coterie. He was far too busy being himself and honest to his convictions (friends aren't always right, and when they're wrong, you've got to tell 'em). With a glory crowd, he would have been fenced and restricted and untrue to his inner self. And he was right.

I watched him long enough one bright, sunny afternoon working with colts to know that his kind of patience would never mistreat an animal. He did it, I think, to show me, an office type, how much could be achieved by kindness. Earlier there had been the halter, then longeing, then the blanket, the bit, and now the saddle. It might have been a tense moment but it was not. In fact, the "breaking" of the colt was carried a step further, just for me. One leg up, the other over, a walk out of the horse lot, then a canter, and finally back to the lot. Without his knowing it, I had some basis for comparison, from the Green River country of Wyoming, where my uncle Big Jim Barrett worked many cattle with many horses, and in Oklahoma, where my own interest gave me access to more than one hundred quarter horses I never rode (I didn't know how). Animals seem to know the people they can trust, and he was right.

From the screened porch at the ranch house near Spearman, he would watch wild turkeys picking their way under the big cottonwoods shading prairie grasses and vines. One hen turkey had hatched out a white chicken (how the egg got into the turkey's nest, nobody seemed to know). At nightfall each evening, crisis arrived. The turkey hen's business was to see that all her young flew high in the cottonwoods, to avoid night-prowling coyotes. But the white chick wasn't equipped for flight. After repeated efforts to induce flight in her white chick, the hen turkey would finally give up and roost on the ground with her charge. The cowman on the screened porch knew what to admire in human character, but also in birds.

The quiet kind sometimes explode suddenly. Our man from Spearman didn't. I had been working on a manuscript one afternoon when he came in, he told me, from the East, where he had been talking with the publisher of his books, some of which were up for reprinting. As the conversation had developed betweent the two, it became clear that this was no environment for a Western cowman with honest convictions about free enterprise, conservative, God-fearing politics, and strong faith in the virtues fulfilled by hard work. The longer the publisher, evidently a politically garrulous man, talked, the more his listener was convinced that he had better take his manuscript and get t'hell out of there. And that was precisely what he did and that was why he had come to Norman. We subsequently published, or republished, all of his books except one on a political subject, earlier mentioned, and some others for which other commitments had been made. And, I'm not boasting in saying, he was right.

Goethe had a saying that "few men have the imagination for the truth of reality." If the truth of reality comes through in the writings of the cowman-historian, it may be that is so no less from his entire familiarity with the land and the people about whom he has written than from his towering gifts as a historian. For in the assessments of literary-historical worth, there has been no disagreement among the informed about *Charles Goodnight: Cowman and Plainsman*, first published in Boston forty years ago. It is the best Plains biography ever written. And, Mr. Haley, this time the critics are right. That I was sure of when you came back from the East to a new publishing house in the West.

6

"HE IS A COWBOY"

by John A. Haley

Many times through the years Evetts Haley has been described as 'the cowboy historian' or 'the cowboy writer' but few I believe really understand what they are saying. The description is apt and accurate but the casual, almost careless, use of the word cowboy by someone who couldn't possibly know the difference is sometimes a little galling to those who do. Just because a man is in the ranching business does not make him a cowboy. It is difficult if not impossible to describe the full meaning of the term, but there is a need so I shall make an attempt.

Simply stated there is only one requirement. He must understand the nature of a cow, and cowboys, like cowhorses, have the basic aptitude bred into them. However, good cowhorses are usually the result of careful selective breeding while the production of cowboys is more haphazard. Which might in part explain the scarcity of good hands.

Cowboys are a class apart. Monetary gain or the spirit-destroying yen for security is no part of their makeup. A cowboy works incredible hours under all sorts of adverse conditions — not only for his employers — but for love of the profession, for the joy of doing a difficult job well. He is also a mass of contradictions. He cusses the weather yet he would starve before taking an inside job. He constantly rages and threatens the life of an obstreperous horse then gleefully relates all his misdeeds to cowboy friends. He will milk a cow to feed a pet cat and notice every interesting thing the cat does; then glumly remark that he wishes the coyotes would catch the damned old nuisance. He is probably the most sentimental creature on earth and would die before admitting it. (Hell! he probably doesn't even know it.)

Though not an avowed student of nature the cowboy has spent his life observing the marvelous fitness of her scheme and delicate balances. He has seen the shattering results when outside forces transgress on nature's omniscient plan and knows intuitively that life itself cannot survive if there is too much tampering with her inviolate laws. He is lucky that he is a cowboy.

Evetts Haley was lucky from the start. The melding of genes was favorable and the makings of a cowboy was born. Evetts, I suspect, withstood the rigors of training better than most. His effervescent nature, tremendous zeal and keen intellect had to have helped during the long, slow, arduous, and often frustrating process of learning the art. And I can well imagine the pride and satisfaction the first time he heard himself called a cowboy, for the term is not loosely used even today. A top hand might say 'he is pretty good', 'nice boy', or 'hard worker' but the simple statement "he is a cowboy" is and always has been the supreme compliment.

Evetts was also fortunate in that he made a good bronc rider and best of all, a more than competent horseman. I once heard another top hand say: "Good horsemen are as scarce among cowboys as cowboys are scarce." These things aren't essential, they are simply bonuses. They make a good cowboy better. However the fine art of roping eluded him. He is only average, and that is an adjective not often used to describe Evetts.

He learned to punch cows in the Pecos River and Midland country where, with youthful fervor and reckless enthusiasm, he worked with some of the finest cowboys of all time. Love of the outdoors and cowboy life became so ingrained in Evetts' nature that even in more recent years he seems to be happiest when fighting a blizzard or drouth. Sometimes though I think this predilection for austere adversity goes too far. Anyone who fights the drouths in Winkler and Loving Counties; blizzards in Hutchinson County; flies, ticks, chiggers, humidity, Arkansas River, Corp of Engineers, and other bureaucracies in Sequoyah County, Oklahoma, by choice is bound to have a problem. I suppose he just loves to fight.

Evetts' ability as a cowboy and a certain amount of business acumen carried him to the height of every cowboy's dream: the running of big outfits. He ran a ranch in eastern Arizona for a while and later was general manager for one of the biggest ranching interests in Texas. But a deep and enduring love of history and the colorful characters who made it, plus an intense patriotism and unyielding sense of duty led him to other pursuits. The success of some of these ventures is evident, others have yet to be evaluated. But one thing is certain, this time spent off the range caused a noticeable deterioration of an always irascible disposition.

My association with Evetts has been — on my part at least — more than avuncular. There is a closeness not easily attained between nephew and uncle with temperaments such as ours. He has, through the years, been immensely helpful and unbelievably patient with a mind much slower than his own. Therefore it is fervently hoped that the next time the reader sees a reference to "the cowboy historian" he will have a little better picture of the man, for Evetts is a cowboy.

7

HALEY: HE'S KNOWN IT ALL

by Gerry Burton

Tales of yesterday roll off his tongue with all the color of a cowboy who has known it all — blizzard, drought, stampede, roundup, deep loneliness, crowded space, and wide-open land.

His face shows the crinkles that come from years of squinting into the sun or against the dust, snow and rain.

A tale in the spinning catches the listener into its midst until the cold or heat, pathos or hilarity floods the mind — and the time is yesterday inhabited by buffalo hunters, cattle barons, rustlers, bank robbers and gentle women.

He is J. Evetts Haley, an avid historian of the life he and others before him have lived and a believer in putting his convictions down as they are, not necessarily as a reader or listener would prefer.

The Canyon rancher-historian, well-known figure around Lubbock in times past, has been in Lubbock more frequently since the publication of *The Flamboyant Judge*, a historical work he co-authored with Dr. W. C. Holden. The memoirs of Judge J. D. Hamlin, who saw the Panhandle develop, is the latest in a long line of Haley writings.

Rugged individualist, friend and foe alike call Haley. He is that and more. He knows the history he has lived and garnered from others, what he has written and promoted despite the effect it may have — and he has enjoyed it to the hilt.

Of his life, touched with controversy over a wide area of space and subject, he says simply, "I've had a lot of fun."

He also chronicled a west few knew, traveling many trails to hear it first hand — history captured while it still burned white hot in man's mind.

"There's no breed like them, they were great," he said of the characters who peopled the West Texas frontier he has explored for half a century.

His files bulge with their stories, many still in interview form, tales spun long ago from full hearts into a thirsty ear.

Rancher, researcher and writer of history, Haley has known the cowboy life of this century and talked to those who lived it before him. His writings have touched outlaw and lawman, rancher and nester, destroyer and builder with equal candor, condemning none. More than 200 books and articles have come from his prolific pen.

The psychology of the times is a thing he wonders about but has never put down. He did ask why of those who lived through the turbulent times. There was the outlaw feeding off the edges of civilization as it pushed west. Looking back in mature years, some who survived the violence of the day told Haley they "did it because it was fun — a great time — high adventure." To the others, "the ones killing them off, it was something they had to do to protect property," Haley said.

Of peace officer Jeff Milton — subject of Haley's *Jeff Milton, a Good Man With a Gun* — Haley noted that Milton considered killing an outlaw his moral duty. "He never shot a man unless the man shot first," he said of the lawman who admitted to being a little afraid when facing an outlaw in a shootout — but only of what he would have to do to the man. Milton also admitted to getting over that feeling after the outlaw had shot at him a couple of times. "When you get to the point where something has to be done, if you're a man, you're going to do it," Haley said, taking in all who did what they had to do to tame the west.

"Head and shoulders above any of the others" Haley came to know was Charles Goodnight — "a great man of terrific vital character, tremendous physical prowess, incomparable courage and moral courage along with it — a philosopher." Haley dedicated the book to his father, "strong-willed battler for his friends and his convictions" and his mother, "frugal, energetic and courageous" whose "old-fashioned virtues sent them west and enabled them to stay." Haley reflects characteristics he attributes to both.

The parents — John A. and Julia Evetts Haley — had started west when Haley was born in 1901. They had reached Runnels County, but Mrs. Haley went back to Belton for his birth. They tried Sterling and Nolan Counties before going to Midland in 1906. The mesquite prairies in Nolan County and a first cattle drive roaring right past his Midland home stand out in his memories of being five. He was to see other herds, larger and wilder, when his folks bought a big ranch on the Pecos River at Pope's Crossing four years later. There he got "a first taste of cattle" watching the "big herds coming up from the Big Bend heading into New Mexico, to ship out at Bovina and Clovis."

The next Haley venture — a big irrigated farm on the Concho River — "broke" the son of farming. He isn't sure if that was the time he decided to be a cowboy, but he knows it was the time he realized that cotton-raising was not for him. Back in Midland County, on a ranch still in the family today, young Haley became a working cowboy. "In 1914 I went to punching cows in the summer, but they kept me herded into school pretty good. There was day work for roundups here and there that sometimes paid a dollar and a half a day."

In the summer of 1916 he "made a hand" full time, getting $16 a month working "seven days a week, from before daylight to after dark." He saved most of that first $16, but the second month he "bought a pair of leggings" as protection from mesquite thorns that had put "Big old knots" on his legs. He paid $14 for the "Batwing style chaps, handmade in a saddle shop by an oldtime German saddlemaker." They now have a home in the Canyon museum. "I was the proudest thing of them, took care of them, too. They would fill with wind and blow out, creating quite a sight."

"We had pride in our work," the cowboy-historian commented. "We were a proud people, a thing not too easy to find today. It wasn't the dollar and a half that kept us at it. We loved it." Haley still loves it, keeping it his life work while getting a broad education and publishing on the side. His education he lays at the feet of a mother who kept pushing him toward it even while he leaned the other way.

Midland College — "A Christian denomination school" — closed after two years and his mother urged him to go to school at Canyon, where a knowledge of history sparked a lifetime love affair with yesterday. It was to grow through a cowboy life and historical research and writing for more than half a century of calm and controversy in many areas including education and politics. History held him with a tight rein for a while. Tracks he made then still show in materials gathered for both the Canyon museum and the University of Texas where his yen for history solidified as he worked on his master's degree.

An overpowering love of land drew him back to it. He accepted "the challenge and exactions of this rigorous land, where God is more manifest in His element wrath than in His benedictions," he wrote about in *The XIT Ranch of Texas and the Early Days of the Llano Estacado.* He managed huge cattle empires and built up his own ranches. He broke his own horses and was a pretty good hand with sourdough biscuits and chuckwagon cooking. Though Haley stayed with the land, he took side roads into research when the occasion and the characters came handy.

He had a way of bringing out life, of getting the core of things missed by others. Perhaps it was his approach to life and the way he had lived it. He could "talk a little bit" about the old times and oldtimers opened up, responding to the vernacular, the look in his eyes, the set of his jaw.

Haley's face shows, in wrinkles going against the normal line, the marks of a stampede that "boogered" him some, chipping vertebrae, caving ribs, ripping off his clothes, tearing flesh from his lower face. His eyes show the determination with which he held his flesh together with a towel from the chuck-box while riding 60 miles in a pickup to the nearest town and many more miles on a plane en route to a doctor he knew could patch him up. A week later "all wired together," he presided at a meeting of the Panhandle Plains Historical Society and flew to a friend's graveside to deliver a eulogy. Two weeks later he was lecturing at a writer's conference at an Oklahoma university.

The same determination saw him facing odds and pursuing unpopular courses through the years because "a man has to be true to his beliefs."

Unpublished history is his main concern now. Interviews from way back when he "threw a bedroll in a Model T and took out" to find history wherever it happened to be mingle now with later research materials in the books that must be done so that history can breathe again.

There's the story of the cowboy with a leaning toward mavericking who was propelled headlong into New Mexico outlawry, with shots from an irate rancher's gun rushing him on his way one dark night in "the Brazos country east of the Matadors."

There's the story of Texas fence wars told by those involved.

There's the tale of a modern bankrobber caught, not by his own mistakes, but by a loan repaid with marked ransom money. There's an endless list of people, places and things and a time that was and never will be again. There's history — unvarnished and plain as the wrinkles on a cowboy's face. It all waits in the files of Haley notes and interviews — waiting the look into yesterday and the set of the jaw to bring it forth.

From the *Lubbock Avalanche-Journal,* Sunday, April 1, 1973, Pp. 1F - 2F.

8

TEXTBOOK TEMPEST: HALEY, DOBIE DISAGREE ON CENSORSHIP

by Richard M. Morehead

Textbooks today are the center of a growing battle in Texas — signifying concern over what goes into the heads of more than two million public school youngsters.

Drawn into the dispute are Texans for America, a conservative group, and the Texas Institute of Letters, opposing censorship of what young people read.

J. Evetts Haley, the leathery rancher from Canyon, heads Texans for America's quest to glorify past heroes and principles of this country and to cut down kind references to the welfare state or world government. Haley is a learned man, whose life has been divided between reading history and writing it, the cow business, and politics.

On the other side is a Texan of similar background, but opposite political view: J. Frank Dobie, white-haired folklorist also rooted in ranch life, has been a star witness for the defence of unfettered reading.

The State Board of Education, local boards, and their professional staffs wrestle with the problem regularly.

A legislative committee led by Rep. W. T. Dungan of McKinney has held lengthy hearings in Austin and Amarillo. The problem which it pointed up has become well known.

Deeply sincere, dedicated people put an unbelievable amount of time, energy and money into volunteer efforts to obtain the kind of textbooks they believe Texas children should have. The differences range from word-picking to vast divisions of political philosophy.

J. Evetts Haley summed up the Texans for America views:

> We believe the primary purpose of basic education is, first, to teach our children how to read, write and use numbers. Second, to transmit facts concerning our heritage, our history and our culture. Third, to develop intelligence and stimulate creative, wholesome thinking. And fourth, provide an atmosphere of moral affirmation without which education is reduced to mere animal training.

Doubtless few folks would disagree with this statement. But in detail, the Haley group runs quickly into opposition.

> I want the textbooks which my children study to be scrutinized objectively and carefully by professionals in the fields concerned," the Dungan committee was told by Frank Wardlaw, director of the University of Texas Press and a spokesman for the Texas Institute of Letters.
>
> I do not want these textbooks to be subject to arbitrary attacks by voluntary censors, either from the right or the left, who tend to view their own concepts of history as revealed truth with which the authors of textbooks must perforce agree. . . . Selection of library books should, in general, be left in the hands of teachers and librarians. Some mistakes will undoubtedly be made, but this is a much safer procedure than the selection by pressure groups. . . . Proper home training and the nurturing of sound literary taste are the best answer to the threat that some people think some types of books pose for developing young minds . . .

As buyer of some $10,000,000 a year worth of books for public schools, the state of Texas is one of the biggest customers in the world. Its youngsters reportedly have access through its free textbook law to about as good books as students anywhere. Many spend as much on outside "work books" as their grandparents did buying texts before the state started furnishing books.

The hearings have indicated to this writer that the quality of textbook offerings often leaves considerable to be desired; that the individual teacher is still largely the key to learning, and books are simply tools.

J. Frank Dobie declared that most textbooks are "very dull."

> One reason they are so dull is that the publishers are so anxious to present something that nobody will object to.

While the state's system of selecting books is considered sound by most school and book people, Dobie charges the state board's advisory committee weakens the selections.

The committee, said Dobie, is "dominated by educationalists. These educationalists are executives in the public schools (actually a majority are classroom teachers). Few of them ever read anything beyond Chamber of Commerce proceedings and Reader's Digest waterings . . ."

America's book-publishing revolution leaves school people in a quandary. More and perhaps cheaper books are available to U.S. readers than at any time in history. Classics can be bought in paperbacks for less than a dollar, sometimes. Yet the avalanche of books may often put accents in the wrong places — mediocrity, filth under the guise of "realism," or downright subversion.

A well-educated, financially successful Austin professional man got this correspondent out of bed one night recently to explain for nearly an hour on the telephone why he thinks certain textbook writers are aligned with a Communist plot to destroy America. Dozens, perhaps thousands, more like this man invest much time and money earnestly trying to promote use of textbooks which fit their concept of Americanism.

On the other side, equally dedicated, are Texans who feel this is the "closed mind" approach, and that public school children should be told about communism, socialism, and the United Nations in a uncritical way. Many citizens consider both groups "extremist" or even "crackpots." Significantly, however, their members usually come from backgrounds of education, culture and often wealth considerably above the public average. Those most concerned about the content of textbooks, and teaching, cannot be dismissed as ignorant. The controversy fits in with ideological warfare elsewhere. Texans for America, main critics of public school books, are conservatives. Defenders are mostly political liberals. Spokesmen for both groups, however, frequently express a belief that books should be better than they are.

The harried publishing industry is trying hard to keep up with demands for $1,500,000,000 a year worth of books. Its publications range from 35¢ paperbacks to deluxe gift volumes costing over $25 a copy. A million paperbacks are sold daily in the United States, and the industry publishes over 15,000 titles a year, according to *Book Production,* a trade journal.

The State of Texas spends about $10,000,000 annually on books, and public school students add considerably to this total by purchasing disposable work books. Nationally, public school textbooks cost $232,000,000 annually, the New York Times reported recently. More than $100,000,000 a year is spent by college students and other textbook buyers.

The State of Texas has furnished free textbooks in public schools since 1919, after some years of designating books which pupils had to buy. Some citizens seriously believe that the free textbook system should be abolished and the schools should return to the business of letting each student buy his books.

Twenty-three states buy books for school children. In most others, the expense is borne by local districts rather than the taxpayer. In some places, pupils still buy their books. Bookmen say there is little difference in cost among methods of buying. In other words, "Free" textbooks aren't less expensive than any other kind. It's just a difference of who pays the bill.

With knowledge spreading like a mushroom cloud and vast new vistas being opened, textbook publishers face the most drastic changes in history. Some of these will be in manufacturing reading materials. Many will be in content — the area of controversy. Example: Fifteen years ago, explanation of "communism" was almost taboo in classrooms because of un-American connotations. Today, the State Bar of Texas and patriotic organizations are urging that public schools everywhere follow Dallas' example in giving each student a course comparing communism with the American way of life.

While attention has been focused on the philosophical-political fight over alleged leftist tendencies in histories and certain other texts, the Texas Education Agency likewise is being called on to deal with other major problems. The entire school curriculum is undergoing a vast change. So are graduation requirements and teacher-training. Latest to receive attention is the modernizing of administrative mentalities in the public schools, which often lag behind late developments in education, and even behind public opinion. The so-called "progressive education" idea which has grown into disrepute for allegedly emphasizing mediocrity is fading from the scene, but slowly.

Rising in its stead — and requiring textbooks to match — is a new emphasis on excellence in public school training. Despite their shortcomings, public schools today doubtless are educating more students better than at any time in history. Schools also are dealing with social welfare problems which were mostly foreign to school administration in the past. They are struggling with problems at both ends of the intellectual scale — and in the middle.

The accent of quality is most often found in science and mathematics. Here also the textbook publishers find it hardest to keep up. Teachers, too, find it difficult to stay abreast of late developments, which a student may have first learned through newspapers, magazines — or even science fiction volumes.

Right now, high school science teachers and students lack adequate textbooks. Those in use currently are 6 to 10 years old and much of the information is out-of-date. This results partly from the state's desire for economy — knowing that new textbooks are being prepared for beefed-up courses in biology, physics and chemistry.

Textbooks have failed — as perhaps they always shall — to keep up with the daily requirements of learning. The State of Texas is trying paperbacks in an effort to meet its textbook needs within the budget. Looseleaf textbooks may be in the offing.

The dispute over histories and related books is a part of the educational problem that receives the most publicity and off-campus attention. The issue is important. So are many other problems facing the public schools on which Texans spend $750,000,000 a year, giving more than 2,000,000 youngsters about as much learning as most of them are willing — or able to absorb. This much is certain:

Public interest in the schools is desirable and usually helpful. Through criticism comes improvement.

9

~

A FEW WORDS ABOUT
BOOK COLLECTING
AND FRIENDSHIP

by Don L. Bradshaw

From the time I started to school until sometime in high school books caused me nothing but trouble, and to say I loved them would have been somewhat inaccurate. I had a special dislike for algebra and geometry books. The only kind I could tolerate at all were history books and even then preferably ones dealing with the southwest and Texas.

Sometime during my high school years I was called upon to read a book of my choice and make a book report. For some reason I choose a book by somebody named J. Evetts Haley, of whom I had never heard. And then, wonder of wonders, I checked out the other Haley books available in the library and read them all *just because I wanted to*. But worse, to further worry me about myself, I started saving money and buying all the Haley books then in print. Never having heard of a rare book dealer, I naturally assumed that if the local book store didn't have it, it didn't exist. Little did I realize.

I read them all two or three times, put them up, married started raising a family and making a living.

A number of years later, I suppose it must have been around 1960, two good friends, Clem Barnes and Joe Mabee, generously invited me to lunch one day. In due course, after several martinis, they apprised me of the fact that they had engaged someone from Dallas to speak in Midland and that their friend J. Evetts Haley had agreed to be present to introduce him. It seemed they had everything necessary for the program with the exception of a place to hold it. After a few more martinis they decided that, as they were both far too busy, maybe I'd better go home, put on my suit, and appear before the school board that afternoon to request the use of one of the school auditoriums. I've never been quite sure whether it was the martinis or the prospect of meeting J. Evetts Haley that prompted me to do it since the idea of speaking before a large group appeals to me about as much as an electric chair. I don't remember now, just as I didn't remember that afternoon, what I said, but we got the use of the auditorium.

I then settled back and began to look forward with great anticipation to the time when I would see and hear and perhaps even meet J. Evetts Haley.

And meet him I did — and I wasn't too sure I was glad. After the program, both the speaker and Mr. Haley were swamped with visitors, admirers and well-wishers. I was at the back end of the line, naturally, and just as I got near Mr. Haley, he turned away and walked back up on the stage — probably to get his hat. Determined to accomplish my purpose on that particular occasion, I followed him, introduced myself, told him I had four or five of his books and wondered if he had ever written anything else. He muttered something to the effect that he had written a few more things, but that some of them were out of print and kind of hard to find. Not only had he not helped my Haley collecting any, but how, I wondered, could a man who wrote so beautifully, have such a dour personality? It was not until some time later that I learned how recently he had lost his "dear Nita".

Well, I continued to buy all the Haley items that came along and wondered where I could find some more. And then, as providence would have it, I found myself officing just down the hall from Clem Barnes who had aided me in getting an audience with the school board.

When Mr. Haley was in town he most always came by to see Clem. On one such occasion I met them in the hall and Clem re-introduced us. Then, after a while, when he came to visit Clem he would come in and say hello to me. I usually had two or three items that I would ask him to inscribe for me and his visits gradually got longer. I soon learned how wrong my appraisal of his "dour personality" had been. He was a very warm person with a great sense of humor and a superb storyteller.

In time, seeing that I was serious about collecting his writings, he began to bring me little things as he came by. I can't describe my delight at this. It wasn't the fact that they didn't cost me anything, or even that they were almost always items that I didn't even know existed; what really made the strongest impression on me was the obvious fact that he *wanted* me to have them.

I have a letter dated March 31, 1966, which reads in part ". . . Thank you for your letter and for your determination to become a collector of Haley books. I am greatly complimented and under separate cover am sending twelve or thirteen items, most of which collectors and dealers properly label as ephemera. These are with my compliments except as indicated on the enclosed invoice covering items sent on approval. It is virtually impossible for me to charge my friends for books. . . ." The acquisition of twelve or thirteen items at that time probably increased my collection by fifteen or twenty percent and the increase in my desire to have a complete Haley collection was inestimable.

My God! That's ten years ago. But what fun we've had in these ten years. So many pleasant hours spent in visiting an storytelling. Our friendship was growing, as well as my Haley collection.

I feel it necessary to mention that my collection finally reached the point where Evetts could help me no more because he only had one each of the items I needed. It was our great mutual friend, Carl Hertzog, who came to my rescue. While talking to Carl on the phone one day, he inquired as to how my Haley collection was coming along. I replied that it was about complete as I needed only four books, all of which fell in the "rarest of rare" category, and, incidentally, all were designed by himself. He asked what they were and I told him.

A few weeks later Carl was in Midland and invited me by his motel room. After some visiting he walked to his suitcase, dug around in it and handed me the four needed books, asking what I thought they were worth? Not only did I not know, but I was afraid to guess. Carl said he did not know how to price them, but he would discuss it with Evetts and let me know. From then until the time he finally advised me of the price was the most traumatic period of my Haley collecting. But I was determined that, whatever the cost, they would never leave my bookshelf. Without Carl's generosity and understanding, and Evetts' blessings, I'd never have cornered them all, and I'm forever grateful to them both.

Despite the great rarity of those four books and the fact that they completed my collection, it is still the lovely "Ode to Nita" that must be considered my favorite. It is by far the most beautiful thing I have read by J. Evetts Haley or anyone else.

Then there is "The Alamo Mission Bell" by J. Evetts Haley. This episode was pure pleasure for me because, by having a small part in the production of the book, I at last was in on the ground floor and would not have to conduct a great search later. For the first time, I got one "hot off the press," and what a personal delight to see my own name, in print and in a Haley book.

It was he who taught me most about books and book collecting. He also pointed out to me the bare essentials of life — books, beef and bourbon. On another occasion he kind of wondered out loud about the possibility that if a book collector stole a book he needed for his collection it might be a sin the Lord would forgive.

I've sat around campfires with him on his ranches and eaten sourdough biscuits and wild plum butter, both of his making.

I've heard him tell hundreds of tales of life and characters of the west and of cow camps, and am ever anxious to hear new ones, or the same ones again, as he is truly one of the great storytellers of all time.

We've fought numerous political battles together and usually lost, so we're pretty sure we were right. We've been together in battles of another nature and usually won.

Perhaps the only really worthwhile project I've ever been involved in was the coming of the Nita Stewart Haley Memorial Library to Midland. I feel privileged to have played a part in it. It gives me a great sense of satisfaction to watch, with Mr. Haley, the progress of the beautiful new building to house the library which has been his life's work.

And by now my collection is complete with the exception of some ephemeral items. Collecting J. Evetts Haley books has been one of the real joys of my life, but decidedly second to sharing a warm friendship with the great Texan who wrote them.

10

~

A DAY ON THE RANCH
WITH EVETTS HALEY

by J. Carl Hertzog

"Let's go to the Ranch," Evetts suggested, "you can sit on the front porch and read manuscript, just you and the birds." A good idea, no distractions, no telephone, not even electricity. Evetts didn't subscribe to the REA or any other government handout. He just cussed them out and suffered the inconvenience.

For some reason I could never understand why he would invite my criticism — me, the tobacco chewing printer — when he would glare and fume if a qualified editor put one single mark on his deathless prose.

It was a hot summer so I slept on the porch, in the upper bunk. Sometime before daylight I awoke with a loud voice close to my bunk bellering, "Jimmy, get up!" Now my name is not Jimmy, but I got up. "Jimmy" is now Evetts, Jr. but he'll always be Jimmy to me. At the urgence of Evetts, Sr., both Jimmy and Don, a Canyon boy drafted for summer work, went out to the corrals, and Nita started breakfast. I could help her a little, set the table, squeeze the orange juice, and get in the way.

After breakfast Evetts put me on the front porch with the manuscript and the three men went back to the corral to saddle up. I read about half a page and heard dishes rattle. I could help Nita, she could wash and I could dry. Then back to the manuscript. After two or three pages I heard a whirring sound and looked out to see that Nita was mowing the lawn.

Now, I couldn't sit there watching a woman doing a man's work, even if I was supposed to be reading manuscript. After I cut the grass and was marking a query on page four, Don came in and said they were going to prowl the North Pasture and Mr. Haley thought maybe I would like to ride along. Being a drugstore cowboy, I never turned down an opportunity to tag along with the real thing.

After we topped out and found a lone cow on the other side, and fixed a windmill on the way, Evetts decided I should take the cow and her calf back to headquarters. About then I felt hungry and thought it must be lunch time. I looked at the sun to verify my calculations and then checked my watch. It was only 9:30 a.m.!

Instead of pushing the cow and her calf on a diagonal across the pastures we had traversed, I let her go her own way, which was hugging the fence line. At one point we were going down a rather steep incline which abruptly leveled off, creating a gap under the fence. The calf went through leaving me and mama cow on the near side. I didn't see anything else to do but take the cow back to headquarters and leave the calf to its own resources.

When Evetts and the boys came in for lunch sometime later he asked, "Where's the calf?" I told him what had happened. He exploded. But for the first time in my life with this awesome character I talked back to him. "I don't claim to be a cowboy," I retorted, "and besides, you aren't paying me all that much."

That evening I settled down to "reading manuscript." Evetts was out doctoring a sick cow. Nita sat in the rocker, sewing. "Nita," I said, "I have read this paragraph three times and I still don't understand it."

Nita took the script and after studying it intently for several minutes, replied, "I keep telling Evetts he writes his sentences too long."

At that moment Evetts stomped into the room, and I said, "Evetts, we have read this paragraph three times and we still don't get the meaning."

Glaring at us, he picked up the manuscript and read the passage in question. Tossing the manuscript back to me and turning on his heel in disgust, he snorted as he disappeared through the door way, "That paragraph is perfectly clear, why don't you all concentrate?"

11

J. EVETTS HALEY: GENTLEMAN

by Thomas J. Anderson

Mr. J. Evetts Haley is made of the same stern stuff which established constitutional freedom on these shores. He has fought to save our republic from socialism, insolvency and surrender ever since that colossal charlatan, Franklin D. Roosevelt, whom President Lyndon Johnson describes as his "second daddy," first started to sell out to the enemy in 1933.

J. Evetts Haley has waged a long and unrelenting battle against wind and sand and drouth and seen his cattle starve, but he has never taken a cent of subsidy from the Federal Government. But the Supreme Court refused to review the famous Haley wheat case in which Mr. Haley's son was fined for feeding his own non-subsidized wheat to his own non-subsidized cattle on his own non-subsidized farm.

J. Evetts Haley is a former teacher who has waged a 30-year battle against Deweyism and progressivism in education. He has written excellent books of Southwestern history and biography which "read like poetry."

He has been called the Thomas Paine of the Southwest.

When I say he is a gentleman and a scholar, I am not being trite — I mean it. He is a gentleman in the finest sense of the word. The epitome of politeness and good manners, he never insults knowingly. He is a man as sentimental as they come and yet hard as steel; erudite yet anti-egghead; serious yet full of fun. A man who loves life, yet loves duty, honor, country more. Few people I have ever known embody more qualities we have traditionally revered in this country — unconquerable courage, unwavering honesty, unquenchable humor, unswerving patriotism, undying faith.

J. Evetts Haley is a man in the finest sense of the word and in the tradition of our illustrious founding fathers.

12

SOME MEMORIES
OF H. D. BUGBEE

by John L. McCarty

There is deep satisfaction in seeing an appraisal of the work and the worth of a man realized. It is a pleasure this reporter has been privileged to have many times during the past fifty years. In no instance has it been more rewarding than in the case of the late Harold D. Bugbee, the Clarendon artist, the illustrator of newspapers, magazines and books, the painter and the master of drawing. That he was a close personal friend, which whom it was my privilege to share a mutual, professional admiration, renders my satisfaction doubly rewarding. That I should set down something about him, his career and his viewpoints as expressed in years of association and scores of letters, seems an obligation to the growing audience that wants to know more of him. My own rating for his work came first during the late 'twenties, to which he referred as his vintage years for painting. Later, it was materially strengthened when he illustrated books that I had written and newspapers which I edited.

Shortly after his death, agents for various important collectors of art, and notably of Western art, began searching throughout the Southwest for his work. At the time, they found very little, and it generally was in the hands of friends who did not want or did not need to sell. At least three of these had collected much of his work. Two were authors for whom he had illustrated, and one was an official of a large oil company whose firm had used his illustrations. Most of his work was held by the Panhandle-Plains Historical Society Museum at Canyon. Bugbee had worked with the Society for years on an annual retainer and felt the museum should have his entire output. In addition to the murals and historical paintings and drawings he did for the Society, he donated much of his work to the museum. During the breakdown and severe illness which he experienced after the death of his mother, he apparently put his house in order. In the process, he burned some 400 drawings which, according to his widow, Olive Vandruff Bugbee, in some cases had only minor imperfections or mistakes in them. He wanted to be remembered for the finest qualities of his work. Many homes, some of them extremely modest and isolated ranch camps, have small drawings or paintings of his today, and they will have them so long as the owners live. Harold Bugbee made friends. He was extremely considerate and had the polished good manners of his Boston background and the generosity and neighborliness of the Southwestern Plains where he lived from his thirteenth birthday. His appreciation of friends and their acts led him to give little tokens of his appreciation.

The failure of Bugbee's vision virtually forced him to quit his illustrating in both pencil and pen-and-ink. His intense, burning desire to use his strength and time to paint in oils is well known. One also recalls the artist's sincere desire to give the greatest possible return for his employment as Curator of Art at the Canyon Museum during many of his later years. His devoted and constant attention to his father and mother in their last years and illness, which finally led to his own heart attack and complete breakdown shortly after his mother's passing, was an overwhelming example of a man's love and responsibility for his parents. All of these factors limited his output and thereby reduced the amount of work available to collectors and museums that wanted to add his name to their catalogue of great Western artists.

The important things in his professional life were the integrity of his work and his continuous dedication, from boyhood, to painting the people, the animals and the breathtaking places of the Southwest of the period 1850 to about 1920. His work reflected his greatness as a man and as an artist. Today there could be no greater monument for H. D. Bugbee than his own paintings of cowboys, Indians, buffaloes, horses, antelope, western skies and chuck wagons. One of his campfire scenes has been rated as one of the greatest paintings of the subject for all time. His cowboys were painted from sketches made of pioneer men who were his friends. He knew most of them around the Panhandle. He could draw Charles Goodnight so well, because he visited with him through the years and claimed him as a friend. He has generally been rated pre-eminent as a painter of buffaloes. He watched them from Canyon cliff or rode among them or worked with them at the Goodnight ranch throughout his boyhood. Every horse that he painted was a specific horse with a name, a certain color, peculiarities and character that belonged only to that horse.

When he was a lad, his mother, a sensitive New England artist, and his father, H. R. Bugbee, an accomplished musician and one-time member of a world-famous band, brought him to the home-place on which was located the site of Old Clarendon. After learning from his mother, he continued his artistic training in the big cities. He then worked with the old Taos masters, two of them being Hoffman and Dunton, close friends. Except for working on the Bugbee ranch, caring for his parents and serving in the armed forces during World War II, he labored only as an artist.

He was above six feet in height, had thick wavy black hair, blue eyes, and wore boots and a large western hat. He was shy, almost self-effacing, yet a standout in any crowd and on any occasion. He had no affectations and possessed a fine voice and a quiet manner. Everyone regarded him as a strong man. He could ride and work cattle with the average cowboy and did so, both on his own ranch and on those of his neighbors, when emergency help was needed. He was known and loved by the townspeople of Clarendon, who early took pride in his work.

His work had the integrity, honesty and character that come from a detailed, dedicated study of the subject painted. He would permit no lesser effort from himself. He listened patiently and appreciatively as his friends — cowboys, Indians, writers, women who knew the country, ranchers, and others, large and small — offered suggestions or information. He got a big boost when some authentic pioneer gave his approval of a horse or cowboy he had painted. He satisfied these people with the correctness and genuineness of his work to the last detail. He reserved to himself the spirit, character and integrity of each painting. He appraised his paintings much as a discerning trader would judge a horse. If he was satisfied, he left the work to the judgment of time. Perhaps that is why Harold Bugbee is rising to the status I predicted for him almost forty years ago.

Colonel, later General, Ernest O. Thompson, now famous for his work as Adjutant General of the 36th Division and as Railroad Commissioner of Texas, gave Harold his first big show. It was held in the Peacock Alley of the Amarillo hotel in the mid-'twenties. He was then in a period when his oil drawings left something to be desired. His color was intense and hot, but the old ranchers and cowboys who thronged "The Panhandle's Meeting Place" gave their hearty approval. They, of course, did little about buying art. It was there, as a reporter for the Amarillo *News*, that I met Harold and became one of his lifelong boosters. Another booster of his, then, was the late Henry Ansley, famous cowboy columnist and public speaker. Another was J. Evetts Haley, the historian, for whom Harold illustrated so many books.

In 1927, I began selling magazine articles on Western subjects to such magazines as *Ranch Romances*. Harold illustrated them and gained another lifelong advocate in the editor, Fanny Ellsworth. In 1929, with Gene Howe, Wilburn Hawk and others as associates, I became editor and publisher of the Dalhart *Texan*. One of the first community enterprises sponsored by my paper was a one-man show of Harold Bugbee's work. He spent two weeks in our home, did some commissions and sold two or three small paintings. One of these was "The Rabbit," a story-telling painting about three calves and a rabbit spooking one another, in which the rabbit's tracks through the snow indicate his hasty retreat. That was, for me, the beginning of the purchase of scores of Bugbee drawings and paintings. A few months later Harold married Katherine Patrick, the daughter of Mr. and Mrs. W. H. Patrick, Clarendon pioneers. Naturally, Katherine had been one of his most devoted boosters. They spent the second night of their honeymoon trip to Denver at our home in Dalhart. On their first anniversary, we sent them some of the rice they were still shaking from their clothes while at our home.

During the depression years, Harold worked hard at his illustrating and at painting. Clyde I. "Pinky" Price, who operates the Clarendon Press, printed a series of Christmas cards of his cowboy subjects, which had a fine reception over the country. The late George Autry, printer, of Amarillo, himself an artist and one of the best friends the artists and writers of the Panhandle ever had, helped in every way possible to sell Bugbee and his works. He used his drawings at every opportunity. Few artists ever attracted the aggressive and loyal following that the Clarendon artist did in Amarillo.

Several of us had a part in selling the idea of using his illustrations for a series of cattle trail articles by some of the best known writers of the Southwest to Shamrock Oil and Gas Corporation. Then, for years afterwards, with J. Evetts Haley as the author, Harold as the illustrator and George Autry as the printer, the Shamrock Corporation produced a superb Christmas mailing piece for its ever-expanding company.

In 1936, I was editor and associate publisher of *The Globe-News*, after being promoted for seven successful years of editorship at Dalhart. Amarillo's fiftieth anniversary was to be in August, 1938, and a year prior to that date we began work on a Golden Anniversary, 288 page edition of the paper. It carried stories by famous writers and historians and was popular as much for its illustrations as for its comprehensive outline material and old pictures. H. H. Hutson, Ben Carlton Mead and Harold Bugbee did the illustrating, with Harold drawing most of the assignments. Here, for one of the few times in his life, he did humorous illustrations. Once he drew a masterpiece in pencil of a horse, to illustrate a story on mustangs by J. Frank Dobie.

He illustrated so many books, magazines and newspapers during a highly productive period in the nineteen-thirties and early 'forties, that the detailed, black and white work began to hurt his eyes. Then he turned to his oils with a vengeance, hoping to put down in color the beauty he felt. During these years he did at least two outstanding mural jobs. One was for his old time patron General Thompson in the Old Tascosa club rooms of the Herring hotel. It was my privilege to do the writing for the program. Here on a grand scale, once and for all time, he answered the critics who complained that his paintings did not show enough action. In time, the critics came to see, not only that he caught action as well as the best, but that the movement was correct in every detail. His large murals at the Canyon Museum, which he executed along with Ben Carlton Mead to give life to historical scenes, attracted so much attention that they set the stage for the Museum directors to employ him on an annual retainer as Curator of Art. This allowed him to devote the remainder of his life to painting for the museum. The wisdom of the action is now measured in a virtually priceless collection which is being increased by friends of the Museum each year.

Undoubtedly, there will be many stories of his life and work, of his devotion to his art and to the country — its people, its animals and its beauty — to which he dedicated his efforts. Surely, J. Evetts Haley could do a masterful book on this man, one of his closest friends, because Haley can write about his friends with as much or more feeling than about those with whom he disagrees. Olive Vandruff Bugbee, who did so much to make his later years happy and easy as wife and fellow artist, could do a masterful piece on his life. Katherine Patrick Bugbee, his first wife, would have a beautiful and touching story to tell. Boone McClure, Curator of the Museum and Ernest Archembeau, historian and editor of the Society's *Review*, would each have great contributions to make on Bugbee's life and art. It is only a short time until all of this material will become extremely important.

Early in his career Bugbee adopted the habit of illustrating his short, jewel-like letters to his friends, as did Charles M. Russell. Whether he got the idea from Russell or someone else is beside the point. Some of his best pencil, pen-and-ink and watercolor sketches are contained in his letters. In these intimate moments he definitely showed his greatness as an illustrator who had life and action and feeling in his drawings. I have illustrated letters expressing appreciation for each check I mailed him. I am sure that his other close friends and patrons have similar mementos. These should be collected into a volume or volumes. I have selected a series of letters received over a thirty year period that definitely point up his ability to portray action.

These general notes give a sketchy report and appraisal of Harold Bugbee, a great Western artist whose stature grew with each year he lived. Now that his work is done, he is no longer thought of as a Clarendon cowboy artist, a Panhandle illustrator, or a courtly gentleman, but as a fine, sensitive, highly skilled artist who gave the world a documentary of high artistic value, depicting an important period in the history of the Panhandle-Plains of Texas.

From *Southwestern Art*, A Journal Devoted to Recognition of the Arts on the West and Southwest. Volume I, Number 3, published quarterly and copyright 1965 by The Pemberton Press, 1 Pemberton Parkway, Austin, Texas 78703. Pp. 21-27.

13

A TEXAN LOOKS AT LYNDON

by J. Evetts Haley

I have been asked to explain some of the background of
the publication of my latest book, *A Texan Looks at Lyndon*,
which is a study in illegitimate power, and how it came to be
written.

This book was conceived, researched, and published as a
sound, historical study, not as a campaign document. No
group, no organization, and no party has had anything whatever to do with its inception, financing, or circulation. I conceived it, I wrote it, and I alone financed it from the very first
and I'm still financing its publication.

Briefly, in this book, *A Texan Looks at Lyndon*, I have:

1. Set forth the illegitimate pressure and power by which,
in a constitutional republic, Johnson was originally put into the
U.S. Congress as a protege of extreme liberal forces of the
original New Deal.

2. I have briefly set forth the fraudulent nature of his
claim of a distinguished World War II record, and how he

returned to his "plush-lined foxhole" in the House Congressional Building in Washington as a lieutenant commander in the Navy.

3. I have told with irrefutable and unchallengeable proof how he, and his political henchmen, and their confederates stole a closely contested U.S. senatorial election in Texas in 1948; a story with all the tragic aftermath of continued fraud and presumed assassinations.

4. In this book, which is a study in illegitimate power, I have proven the false, the shallow and shoddy nature of the claim that the origin of the Johnson family's multimillion-dollar fortune was founded on his wife's inheritance. It was, instead, laid with the acquisition of a radio and television monopoly in Austin, through the illegitimate use of power to ruin the owner of the station, which fell as an over-ripe plum into Lady Bird's lap, to put her husband and his family on their way to immense wealth.

5. I have detailed the methods, the men and the means by which Government contracts and political favors on one hand, and protection from tax problems and Federal harrassment on the other, were used to enrich Johson's big corporate backers in Texas, like Brown & Root of Houston, while on the other hand oppressing and even destroying those of humble origin and status who, with sufficient character and courage, have resisted his illegitimate power.

6. I have pointed out Johnson's intimate connections with such wheeler-dealers as Billie Sol Estes. One man after another, with intimate knowledge of the fantastic fraud, or with close connections with the principals involved, died sudden, mysterious, and violent deaths, while the profitable, tangible assets of the Estes empire were, without financial risk, handed virtually as a multi-million dollar gift to a friend and supporter of Johnson.

7. In this "Study in Illegitimate Power," I pointed out that a Pecos citizen, a locally prominent, successful doctor who discovered and exposed this gigantic fraud by printing the story in a Texas county newspaper, was ruined financially and professionally, while Billie Sol Estes, with more than $18 million in Federal tax judgments against him and with two prison sentences for fraud imposed by Texas courts, is still free, living in

a plush $50,000 home, driving a 1964 Cadillac, and living high off the hog of political influence.

8. I have again brought attention — with added detail — to Johnson's close connections with Bobby Baker. In this connection, I have presented evidence of his undoubted ability in Senator Fulbright's apt phrase — "to manage Congress" — and to suppress any inquiry anywhere on Capitol Hill, from that of Billie Sol Estes to Bobby Baker.

9. I have factually detailed the ruthless, vindictive and dangerous nature of this power-mad man, elevated through malevolent fate into the most powerful office in America's history. All I have done is to bring my years of knowledge of the Texas scene and my ability as an academic investigator and historian to dig deep into the intimate and reliable sources of information. Having done this, I stand unafraid of what may follow — even the most ingenious and most effective technique that illegitimate power has historically invoked — because I believe in the sanctity of the printed word, well-knowing that when I commit the honest judgments of history to the printed page, they are for the author, whether fortunate or hapless, beyond recall.

The foregoing statement was issued by Mr. Haley at a press interview in Los Angeles, California, September 1, 1964. It is reprinted from the *Congressional Record*, September 1, 1964, pp. A4550-A4551.

14

SUPPRESSION OF A BOOK

by Joseph Warren

"Modern man rejects everything that reason cannot understand and destroys with an epigram the inarticulate wisdom of the centuries."

—*Voltaire*

During election year 1964 J. Evetts Haley's book *A Texan Looks at Lyndon* became a national best-seller almost overnight; perhaps enjoying the greatest number of sales in any similar period of time in history.

This 254 page paperback had no advance publicity. Haley had researched, written and published his expose of Lyndon Baines Johnson and his cronies as a factual historical study, all at his own expense. The initial printing was 100,000 copies and distribution was begun in late June by a few friends and conservative bookstores.

The response was spontaneous. People were soon asking, "Where can I buy a copy?" and "Have you read *that book* about Lyndon?" Copies in early circulation quickly became dog-eared by being passed from hand-to-hand. In a short time there were four printing houses turning out thousands of copies and even they could not keep up with demand.

The news media ignored the explosive little volume until sales were well into the millions. Texas papers with long-established book review sections featuring Texas authors carried no mention of it. The first press reference to Haley's *Study in Illegitimate Power* was a four-line "Minor Memo" in the *Wall Street Journal* on June 26, 1964. *The Dallas Morning News* briefly mentioned it as a best-seller on July 7th. On the previous day, an Amarillo paper concluded a review of the book by stating that "Historian Haley, who has a dozen books under his belt, uses the historical approach. Incidents are carefully documented in footnotes using a range of sources from newspaper accounts to court records."

July and August sales soared fantastically. The Palo Duro Press, Haley's publication and distribution agency, was, at one time, a third of a million copies behind on its orders. He recruited help largely from students at West Texas University in his home town of Canyon. But it was impossible to keep pace with the demand. On September first, just two and one-half months after the first copy appeared in print, Haley, with four presses in production, announced that a total of 7,250,000 copies had either been sold or were on order with his printers.

Mounting sales soon forced Democrats and the occupant of the White House to take notice of *A Texan Looks at Lyndon*, and the evil tactic to destroy a book by discrediting its author got underway. A Democratic brochure attacking the book was distributed as a campaign document. Commentators on radio and television exploded in a broadside of vituperation. The drive to smear Haley proliferated into thousands of letters and articles picturing him as a "bitter failure," a man capable only of "invective, festering hate and frustration" and, according to A. C. Greene in the *Dallas Times Herald*, "a case of unhospitalized paranoia."

Governor John Connally was interviewed and dismissed the book as "scurrilous." Johnson-Humphrey Headquarters took official notice of it with labels such as "trash," "evil," "charming little hate-book," and so on.

Ronnie Dugger in his *Texas Observer* charged that the book was a piece of "rumor-mongering." Paradoxically, much of the documentation of *A Texan Looks at Lyndon* was taken from the press itself. Of the 225 newspaper references used, Dugger's sheet was cited 18 times, more than any other one source.

The crescendo of venom spread mainly from three sources: "The Power of Fantasy" by A. C. Green in the *Dallas Times-Herald* "The Voice of Many Hatreds" by Jim Mathis in *The Houston Post*; and, a syndicated column by Drew Pearson in which he accused Haley with having connections with the American Nazi Party. At a well-attended press and television interview in Dallas in late September, Evetts refuted these diatribes. "Once again," he said, "Drew Pearson has adopted the communist technique of the big lie through guilt by association. I have never seen, met, written to or talked with anyone in the Nazi Party, nor have I ever had any patience or sympathy with that movement."

The networks did not pick up the refutations. Haley and the Palo Duro Press were besieged with letters and phone calls asking for answers to the defamatory charges. But Haley simply had neither the time nor sufficient help to answer each inquiry individually, so the public was left to wonder. Lie after lie was printed, enlarged upon and reprinted. It seemed that the news media's only interest was in printing and amplifying the smear.

Among the few exceptions, however, was the prestigious *Chicago Tribune*. On October 16, Walter Trohan, in an article entitled "Texan's Book on Johnson is Still at Top," said, "Haley's detractors have made no attempt to answer his charges. Instead they have centered their fire on Haley, calling him a hate-monger and a crackpot in published reports and worse in whispering campaigns."

The Houston Post articles by Jim Mathis were by far the most vicious. Ignoring the book completely, Mathis excoriated the West Texan as the "voice of many hatreds." In answer, another newsman, Ted Lewis, in his column "Capitol Stuff," said:

"Mathis is a reputable newspaperman but in this case he could be prejudiced. His wife is the daughter of George Brown of the fabulous Brown and Root firm which has had billions in big defense contracts and it was on a visit to Brown's hunting country estate that LBJ suffered his heart attack."

It is interesting to note that Mathis met the Brown heiress when they were both working for *The Houston Post*. In a short time Mrs. Mathis and the children showed up in Reno. After the divorce, Mathis married the Brown daughter.

"The Voice of Many Hatreds" begins with a half-column of Faustian hyperbole describing Haley's home section, the Llano Estacado: "The land and its climate imprints itself upon the people . . . now and then they toss up a spokesman who takes upon himself all the misfits, the unredeeming hatreds and hopeless prophecies . . . such a man is J. Evetts Haley. (He) has moved away into a rocky netherland of hate." Mathis misquotes J. Frank Dobie as having said: "He (Haley) is a mean fighter — he hates, hates, hates." But Robert Sherrill, who himself authored a diatribe against Haley, gives the correct quote in *The Miami Herald*: "Evetts is sometimes a mean fighter. But I'll say this: if he thinks he's right, he'll stand there all alone in a blizzard and the rain and fight for what he believes in."

Again in "Capitol Stuff," Ted Lewis, referring to these *Post* articles, asks: "But what does this have to do with Haley's printed charges concerning the way LBJ rose to political power? If they are libelous why doesn't someone sue? If they are false what are the actual facts? The Johnson type of technique is being used. Haley must be cut down and discredited. Why doesn't someone just say the *book* isn't true?"

Even the religious press joined the hue and cry. Dr. E. S. James, editor of *The Baptist Standard*, condemned the book as "totally out of place in a Christian bookstore," and the denomination's Southern Sunday School Board thereupon banned its sale in all Baptist Book Stores. Carl Keithley of the *All Church Press* chimed agreement, further banning, with his epigram, Haley's effort to present truth and facts to the electorate.

As the presidential campaign progressed, pressures were put on dealers and brokers with franchises in the paperback trade. The administrative officers of the Denver Airport, for example, ordered it removed from the terminal. The newstands at Dallas Love Field did not stock it "on orders from New York." News agencies in many of the country's largest cities absolutely refused to handle it. The National Republican organization would not touch it, and Party officials generally avoided the book like the plague. The demand plummeted during the final weeks of the campaign at a time when sales should have been the heaviest. Tremendous printing orders were cancelled, and by late October the demand had been reduced to a trickle. The smear campaign depicting Haley as a crack-pot, a liar and a charlatan had apparently worked despite his reputation as a leading American historian and biographer.

J. Evetts Haley's first book, *The History of the XIT Ranch*, published in 1929, was written for the Chicago interests that built the Texas capitol. Persons named in the book as outlaws filed suit for $2,200,000 libel, but the author and the publishers proved in court that what Haley had written was true and he won the case. The book was re-issued by the University of Oklahoma Press, slightly revised, many years later. The 1929 edition now is a valuable collectors' item.

Many other notable works have come from Haley's pen, classics of the region, recording Texas and Southwestern history. Great writers such as Frazier Hunt, friend and biographer of General MacArthur, praise the cowman's life of Charles Goodnight as the finest frontier biography ever written. Haley's *Fort Concho and the Texas Frontier* won the Summerfield G. Roberts award in 1952 as the best historical work published in Texas that year. Dr. Eugene C. Barker, dean of Texas historians, considered Evetts his most outstanding student. Dozens of magazine articles, brochures and pamphlets carry his signature.

In spite of having spent at least half his adult life in patriotic endeavor, this so-called "frustrated failure" has acquired several ranches which he operates together with his son. He is proud of being a top cowboy, but he is also a cowman, and the terms are not synonymous. The Haleys could have become wealthy by accepting Federal subsidy but instead they fought all the way to the Supreme Court of the United States for the "right to do what I will with mine own" by planting wheat on their own land to feed their own cattle. But the Court decreed that they must pay a fine for so doing.

The Haley library is perhaps the most valuable and important collection of books, files, art and artifacts on Texas and the Southwest outside an educational institution. Hundreds of recorded interviews with oldtimers and people of note greatly enhance the historical value of this collection. Now known as the Nita Stewart Haley Memorial Library, it is permanently housed at Midland.

The late J. M. West, Sr., the largest individual ranchman in Texas, employed Haley as manager of his ranching interests, as did W. E. Wrather of Dallas, and L. L. Dent, movie chain magnate who ranched extensively in Arizona, New Mexico and Colorado.

In 1951, addressing The Panhandle-Plains Historical Association, Dan Casement, Princeton graduate, scholar, eminent cattleman and proud son of General Jack Casement who built the Union Pacific, said: "I have known and greatly admired for many years your President, Evetts Haley. He is one who measures up fully to my conception of a complete man. He has enriched our literature by valuable biographies of great men of the West who walked the earth in simpleness and honor and clean mirth. The products of his pen reflect his sound common sense, his fine appreciation and deep understanding of human nature."

Mr. Casment has aptly described the man who tried to tell the truth to America. The hand-wringing liberals and the prostituted press, engineers of Lyndon's Great Society, suppressed the book by defaming the author, but no statement in *A Texan Looks at Lyndon*, nor any conclusion drawn from its well-marshalled facts, was ever challenged by the President, his friends or his idolators.

116

15

MEMOIR ON J. EVETTS HALEY

by Joe B. Frantz

While I was still a teenager a group of women in Weather-
ford formed a reading group within the local branch of the
Federated Women's Club. They bought one book a month,
everyone read it, and at the end of the year, they divvied up
the books. My older sister, Josephine, drew J. Evetts Haley's
Charles Goodnight, which I believe was a Literary Guild selection. I doubt that she ever read it, but I did.

During the second World War I was on destroyer duty in
the Pacific when my wife sent me a copy of Haley's *George W.
Littlefield, Texan.* Again I read a book by Haley.

Despite my callow political outlook I had also become
aware that Haley was controversial, because The University of
Texas had not renewed his contract as a gatherer of materials
for its archives. The separation left intimations that Haley's
flirtations with the Jeffersonian Democrats and the Liberty
League in particular and his anti-New Deal sentiment in general

were responsible for the non-renewal, although the University countered that in the middle of the Depression it simply lacked funds to continue the luxury of a field man for archives. But the anti-Roosevelt forces felt that they had found an articulate martyr, an item that the University has furnished freely and regularly to persons of all sorts of persuasions over the generations. Haley was the 1936 nominee for canonization.

Evetts first slipped into my consciousness as a flesh-and-blood human being at one of the early annual meetings of the Texas State Historical Association. Thomas R. Havins, professor of history at Howard Payne College, was scheduled to read a paper dealing with range history in Brown County. En route to the meeting, he was intercepted by a call that his daughter was having an emergency appendectomy, but somehow forwarded his paper to the appropriate people, after which he returned to his daughter's side.

The director of the Association, H. Bailey Carroll, asked Haley to read Havins' paper. This long lean booted figure with a voice so typically Texan that not even Hollywood could have matched it uncoiled himself and faced the audience. He was good-looking, erect, with the clear blue eyes of a man who had found his place in the world. He began to read, and his voice fascinated me. But about the third sentence he interrupted himself:

"Now I don't agree with that," he said about Havins' first paragraph. Then he proceeded to tell why.

From then on the Havins session consisted of one paragraph by Havins and two oral rebuttal paragraphs by Haley. A 25-minute paper stretched into an hour to an hour-and-a-half. Havins' thoughts almost got lost in the process. Most of us envied his being there at his daughter's bedside instead of in the room with us. The performance was at moments hilarious, for no one can speak with more verve and color than Evetts. You know that he is authentic, that the words come straight from the feedlot and the pasture, that here is one of those rare writers on the west who knows intimately what he is talking about. But then outrage crept into your soul as you thought of what he was doing to Havins, who was not there to defend himself, not to mention what he was doing to you as an auditor.

Carroll and some of the older hands were outraged by Haley's breach of manners. My own feeling has been that in a third of a century of attending Texas State Historical Association sessions, he gave it one of its few memorable moments in a long panorama of papers that are mainly bland and easily forgettable. I would have to call it a prize performance and vintage Haley, and I have cherished the memory ever since.

When Haley ran for governor in 1956, he held a rally at the old Pease mansion under the loose sponsorship of the late Niles Graham, a bit of a character himself. Walter Prescott Webb, who had no use for Haley's politics but great admiration for Haley as a man, attended the rally. The next morning he told me, "I disagreed with almost everything that Evetts said last night, but I'll tell you one thing, he's the only honest man in the race!" With integration of public schools as a key issue at the time, Evetts let it be known that he favored the resurrection of legal interposition, a doctrine that Andrew Jackson presumably disposed of a century-and-a-quarter before when John C. Calhoun in South Carolina had gotten contrary. If the courts and the government wouldn't go with interpositions, then Evetts promised to meet any federal marshals as they crossed the border into Texas and turn them back at the point of a pistol. No one doubted but that he would give it a good try. Talk about Lyndon Johnson and an Alamo complex! Johnson was a marshmallow alongside Haley.

One other time I was with Webb when he expressed his admiration of Haley. Haley had just been stumping politically, madder'n hell about some issue, and a little covey gathered to damn Haley from here to Canyon. In the midst of the collective philippics Webb, who could stand extremism in anyone except himself, suddenly stopped the conversation with, "You fellows can say whatever you want to about Evetts — he still makes the best biscuits of any man I've ever known!" Obviously, to Webb, a man who could bake good biscuits in a Dutch oven was not a man to attack for mere political views.

When Eugene C. Barker died, Evetts, who almost occupied a position as Barker's foster son, was naturally a choice for a pallbearer. As usual, I was the last pallbearer to show up at the funeral chapel. When I arrived, I could hear a low hum. In his usual unctuous manner the funeral director showed me the room where the pallbearers were foregathering. As I approached, the hum grew into a minor roar. Inside, I discerned why. Haley was up in some older fellow's face, shaking his finger and talking loud and non-stop, the only way he apparently knows how to talk.

After the funeral a group of us went to the Night Hawk to soften our bereavement with coffee and chocolate icebox pie. Haley was morose and silent. We reminisced about Barker casually, as men do when an influence has moved on. About twenty minutes into our conversation Haley stretched himself slowly, like a dog waking in the morning, and said quietly, "Gentlemen, I want to apologize for my behavior this afternoon. I had no business talking like that. I loved the Chief, and would never do anything to dishonor his memory, But —," and he leaned forward, "I had been waiting to get that damned judge in my sights." And for the next twenty minutes Haley delivered a blistering monologue against that same pallbearer, now happily absent, who turned out to be Judge Hutcheson, Barker's brother-in-law. It seems that Hutcheson, a federal judge in Houston, had delivered an opinion that Haley interpreted as coddling the liberals, and Haley had been burning the grasslands up there above the Cap Rock with his distaste for Hutcheson ever since. A man with real venom, so it seems, spits it out whenever he gets the opportunity, even at the funeral of a man he probably revered more than any other.

After his gubernatorial experience Evetts pretty well avoided Austin. Years went by without his ever attending another annual meeting of the Texas State Historical Association. Then in 1961 I was driving to San Francisco when on the first evening out, dusk overtook me at Canyon. I checked into a motel and called Evetts. With obvious cordiality he invited me out to his house and gave me good directions. When I arrived, he grasped my hand warmly, asked how I drank my coffee, and was geniality itself.

Before the conversation got too far along, I said pleasantly enough, "We've been missing you down in Austin, Evetts."

"Oh, you sons-of-bitches! I don't want to ever have anything to do with a bunch of lily-livered bastards like you! The fact that one of you hasn't shot anyone is proof enough to me that you've no character, because several of you sure need shooting."

And then he was off. For forty-five minutes he talked, ripping people and politics apart, not caring to ascertain which side I was on nor whether any of the people were my friends. I just sat there and listened, fascinated by the torrent of words. And then suddenly he pulled up, gave me that irresistible grin of his, and said with a complete change of pace, "You know, fellow, it has been wonderful visiting with you tonight. I hope you never come to Canyon without dropping by to see me."

I went out into the night feeling rather reassured. The world might be coming apart right in front of my eyes, values might be changing, all sorts of unseen forces might be at work, but Evetts was like the rock that standeth by the water. He didn't move, he didn't change. Even a rock erodes, softening its contours with time, but not Evetts. His edges remained as granite sharp as ever.

A similar experience must have happened to J. Frank Dobie. He and Evetts had been very close, and they shared a lot of the same characteristics. Both were widely read, were good talkers (for my taste, Evetts was better), and were equally capable of expressing dogmatic opinions, although almost invariably on opposite sides of an issue. But over the years as their political tendencies drifted — or raced — toward opposite poles, each said things about the other's character and mentality that left no room for friendly retreat. Gradually all contact was dropped, and for all practical purposes they quit speaking. This worried many of us, for we believed that opinions should not get in the way of friendship, that the men we treasured were bigger than that. But Evetts was 500 miles away, so that distance made him a lost cause. Since Frank Dobie was in our backyard, we talked to him about the breach.

When in the midst of our apparently abortive advisings Evetts' first wife died, Mrs. Dobie urged Frank to write Evetts a letter of condolence. He did. Included was what for someone else would have been a perfunctory sentence that ran something like this, "The next time you're in Austin, let's get together." Evetts knew that Frank was not being casual. Dobie was extending an olive branch, and Haley accepted the proffer.

So the next time Haley was in Austin, he called Dobie, and jsut the two of them went to lunch together. I don't have Evetts' side on this, only Dobie's. According to Dobie, Evetts delivered one of his monologues in which he bruised every tender spot in Dobie's makeup. If Dobie were sensitive on an issue, Evetts drilled right straight into the sensitivity without any nerve gas or other leaven. According to Dobie — and his friends find this statement, if true, borders on the miraculous —, "I kept my mouth shut and never disputed a word he said. We did not fight; I just let him talk."

But then Dobie said to me, "I never intend to see him again if I can avoid it. We have buried the hatchet, and we'll let it stay buried. But there's no meeting ground any more for us."

As long as he stayed off politics, Evetts had an engaging sense of humor and a devastating phrase-making ability. One that followed Dobie through the years was stated when a group of us were talking about Dobie's erratic driving habits. Said Evetts: "Frank doesn't drive a car — he just loose herds it!" Dobie never lived down that phrase.

The time when we more craven rationalists decided that Evetts was irretrievably lost occurred during one of those periodic witch hunts that the Texas legislature stages to purge its soul for the edification of its constituents. Such occasions could be considered high comedy if an underlay of sinister possibilities didn't accompany them. But on this occasion the legislature was making itself ridiculous again by investigating the Americanism of textbooks adopted by the Texas public schools. A committee ran a traveling roadshow under the leadership of a pious fundamentalist from Grand Saline named Bill Hollowell. The show played in various towns, almost always to the same types of people with the same witnesses. Some freshly scrubbed 14-year-old kid opined as how he hadn't encountered an honest textbook written since 1883. Some gaggle of women who had lost touch with reality wanted a textbook voided because it gave more attention to Franklin Roosevelt than it did to Warren G. Harding (which probably was a break for Harding). At the end of each session Evetts was almost always present to point out the weaknesses in the arguments of the pro-textbook witnesses, to suggest flaws in their character, and in general to act like a cross-examining attorney. Almost every publisher's representative and academic type was vulnerable in some respect, insofar as the committee was concerned, as Evetts revealed that the witness was not a regular church-goer, had never sung in the choir, had once signed a precinct petition for Henry Wallace, had attended Harvard, or something equally obscene.

When at last the summit meeting of the committee was held in Austin, some officials from the Texas Institute of Letters had the inspiration of inviting Dr. Joseph M. Dawson, whose name was almost synonymous with the Southern Baptist Church in Texas, to come along as a witness. Dawson has edited the *Baptist Standard,* had been on Baylor University's Board of Trustees, had held a leading Baptist pastorate in Waco for a third-of-a-century, had been an official of the Southern Baptist Convention, and on and on and on. John the Baptist hardly could produce more credentials as a Christian gentleman or as a member of that specific denomination.

When Dr. Dawson, a frail saintly-looking old gentleman in his 80's, testified, he was told by committee members that one of the complaints against a text was that it failed to make clear that the United States was a Christian nation. Dr. Dawson retorted that of course ours was not a Christian nation, never had been, was not now, and possibly would not ever be. He observed that he had spent more than 60 years trying to make Christians out of Americans, that he had enjoyed considerable success, but that as much work remained to be done as when he had begun.

Chairman Hollowell and the others of the committee could hardly believe their ears. If the United States is not a Christian nation, then what is it, they inquired. Dr. Dawson was ready:

"It is a nation of free men, free to be Christians or not to be, free to be Baptists or Catholics or Jews or Mohammadans or atheists or whatever they choose," answered the frail octogenarian. The galleries, filled largely with University of Texas at Austin students and faculty, applauded, and the Texas Institute of Letters types smiled at their genius in selection. They thought that the committee had been destroyed.

But before the conclusion of the meeting Evetts was asked if he had anything to say. He arose, while the Texas Institute of Letters members thought that for once they had silenced him. He began to attack J. Frank Dobie as a Communist fellow traveler and as an evangelical atheist, along with a few other intimations. He tore the other witnesses apart. But the TIL people knew that attacking Dr. Dawson was tantamount to attacking Jesus himself. After Evetts had carved up every other pro-textbook witness, he came to Dawson:

"Now we come to that so-called Baptist, Dr. Joseph Dawson of Waco. . . ." The TIL people knew then that the cause was hopeless. Dr. Dawson a so-called Baptist!

Evetts had again carried the day.

During the campaign of 1964 Evetts got involved with the right wing of the Republican party as a result of his book, *A Texan Looks at Lyndon.* I saw the book in Republican bookstores, sometimes filling the whole window displays from Denver to Dulles airport. Reputedly it was selling more copies than any other book ever printed except the Bible. The John Birch Society virtually made it compulsory devotional reading for its membership and for school kids who wouldn't be voting yet for another four or five years but whose salvation should begin right now.

Undoubtedly publication figures were inflated, as was revealed when a San Antonian sued Haley for allegedly using some of his writings without permission. The size of the judgment, if there were any, would doubtless be based on how widely the book had been distributed. The result was that the trumpeted sales figures tumbled from the millions to around three-quarters of a million, still a highly desirable figure but more in the class of Wendell Wilkie's *One World* than in the company of St. Luke and St. John.

J. Pat O'Keefe, secretary to the executive council of the Texas Democratic party, with offices in the Brown Building in Austin, liked to tell how he was going up to his office on the elevator one day. Aboard with him was one of those sweet little lady worker types who had a book with her thumb stick in it like a wiener in a hot dog bun, obviously keeping her place until she could get back to her desk. Pat looked closer and saw that the book was Haley's *A Texan Looks at Lyndon.* Since the woman knew Pat and knew also that he worked for the Democratic party, she smiled at him, glanced at the book, and said softly, "I'm reading everything I can about our wonderful leader in Washington." Pat would have preferred that she read less.

Every Texan knows that the moving spirit behind the Panhandle-Plains Historical Society and the Panhandle-Plains Museum in Canyon from its inception almost to the present has been J. Evetts Haley. He gave the museum its collection and he gave the *Panhandle-Plains Review* what you are supposed to give your church — your gifts, your presence, and your prayers. But a few years ago democracy, bloc-fashion, overtook the Panhandle-Plains Historical Society. Friends of former state senator Grady Hazlewood from Amarillo, less than 15 miles from Canyon, decided that their man should become the new president of the society. Quietly they organized and showed up at the annual meeting in a group, with the obvious numerical ability to carry the day.

Now Evetts had never tried to set any continuity records as president of the society, but he had always seen to it that the right people were named as officials. Here was a threat. Evetts got the floor and began a long speech, most of it factual though basted generously with emotion, about how he had never dictated to the society but had always hoped that the best man would win. The fact that the best man had always been a friend of Evetts' was not mentioned. Before Evetts was through, Senator Hazlewood's lawyer had been dislodged from his chair by a fist from Evetts' son, pandemonium had ensued, and a new breed (though not a gentle breed) had taken over the reins of the society.

Not directly connected, but still a spinoff, is the somewhat sad sequence in which Evetts later came over to the Panhandle-Plains Museum and removed his collection, which was the museum's backbone. An entity which he had supported generously for a decade had now become off-limits for even his inanimate holdings.

As I said, we had not seen Evetts in these parts since he ran for governor. I had tried to interview him once when I was running an oral history program wrapped around the life and career of Lyndon B. Johnson. He had scrawled across my request a big NO, initialed the refusal, and sent it back without comment.

But a couple of years ago we asked him to spend a day with the Institute of Texas Studies group which the Texas State Historical Association and The University of Texas sponsor each year. He accepted.

It was a delight to have him around. I rather felt that he expected the students to protest his presence and he came in a bit of a defensive posture, but of course student generations are short and their memories are transitory, and to today's student he was as much a historical figure as Governor James Stephen Hogg or Jack Johnson would have been. Time had dispersed and defused the controversy. Evetts put in a whole day with the students and in the old vernacular, he turned 'em ever' way but loose. They were enthralled, his complete captives within ten minutes after he started talking. He r'ared back and told how life used to be when the west was spacious and ample and men locally made their own rules. Some critic might have complained that Evetts' picture of the Old West, especially of the cow country, was romantic, that he made it better than it ever was, but to the students, mostly young school teachers taking a refresher, he was the real product, as genuine as a tin of Arbuckle coffee and as redolent of the frontier as the smell of a hot branding iron on bovine flesh. He brought some of the students near to tears. He was beautiful, he was thrilling, he had integrity, he was easily the highlight of the summer, perhaps even of a lifetime. His power to talk was undiminished, and the phrases rolled off his tongue with all the genuineness of seventy years of careful observation. On that day I don't believe there was a narrator in the United States who could have touched him.

What it comes down to is this: Evetts is a little bit akin to a high-spirited fractious pony. He won't stand hitched, he won't play the game, he is just going to be himself and buck and pitch and jackknife whenever he feels like it. On the other hand, in a world in which my colleagues become ever more bland, Evetts brings to life the same sort of authoritative seasoning that red chiles bring to a pot of stew. He seasons the place, gives it life and color. He may raise considerable hackles, but he is like the astronauts talking about the moon. When he talks about the Old West, he has been there. Whether I agree with what he's talking about is almost beside the point. He makes good music with his words, and history and tradition are richer for his presence.

Besides, I'm told that he makes the best biscuits of any outdoorsman in Texas.

16

~

A BIBLIOGRAPHY
OF THE WRITINGS OF

———⟨———

J. EVETTS HALEY

Compiled and Edited By

Chandler A. Robinson

SECTION A

〜

BOOKS AND PAMPHLETS WRITTEN OR EDITED BY J. EVETTS HALEY

Arranged Chronologically

1. *Lore of the Llano Estacado; Cowboy Songs Again.* Austin: Texas Folk-Lore Society, 1927. Wrappers. 25 pages. (The pages of *Lore* are numbered 1-7.) Reprinted from *Texas and Southwestern Lore*, Publication Number VI of the Texas Folk-Lore Society, 1927.

2. *Charles Goodnight's Indian Recollections.* Amarillo: Russell & Cockrell, Inc., 1928. Wrappers. 29 pages. Reprinted from *Panhandle-Plains Historical Review*, 1928, Volume 1, Number 1. 22.6cm × 15.4cm. One hundred copies were printed.

3. *The XIT Ranch of Texas and the Early Days of The Llano Estacado.* Chicago: The Lakeside Press, 1929. Cloth. 261 pages. Map. Frontispiece. Photos. Foldout. Acknowledgement. Introduction by John V. Farwell. Poem: "Backward, Turn Backward." Appendix. Bibliography.

Index. 23.4cm × 16cm. The first edition consisted of 1,380 copies, and was withdrawn from circulation soon after it was first issued.

"J. Evetts Haley . . . as one of the small group at Canyon that pioneered in the organization and development of the Panhandle-Plains Historical Society, . . . has contributed perhaps more than any other one individual to the preservation of the history of this section . . . The XIT Ranch of Texas is a monumental work . . . Haley has made his debut as a historian and writer in an impressive manner."
— John L. McCarty, in the
Amarillo News-Globe, 1929.

3b.   New and revised edition. Norman: The University of Oklahoma Press, 1953. Cloth. 258 pages. Photos. Maps. Foldout. Preface. Appendix. Bibliography. Index. Dust-jacket. 23.4cm. ×16cm.

3c.   The Western Frontier Library Edition. Norman: University of Oklahoma Press, 1967. Cloth. 258 pages. 19cm × 12cm. This is volume 34 in the Western Frontier Library.

4.   *Jim East, Trail Hand and Cowboy.* Canyon: Panhandle-Plains Historical Society, 1931. No pagination (24 pages). Wrappers. Illustration by Harold D. Bugbee. Reprinted from the *Panhandle-Plains Historical Review,* 1931, Volume IV. 23.3cm. × 15.4cm.

5.   *A Log of the Texas-California Cattle Trail, 1854.* By James G. Bell. Edited by J. Evetts Haley. Austin, 1932. Wrappers with extended edges. 79 pages. Reprinted from the *Southwestern Historical Quarterly,* Volume XXXV-XXXVI, 1932. 24cm. × 15.6cm. One hundred copies were printed.

6.   *A Log of the Montana Trail as Kept by Ealy Moore.* By Ealy Moore. Edited by J. Evetts Haley. Canyon, 1932. 13 pages. Reprinted from the *Panhandle-Plains Historical Review,* Volume V. 23.3cm. × 15cm.

6b.   Fifty copies were bound in light tan cloth.

"Haley had the printer send me 50 (or 100?) to order the binding done in El Paso; the bookbinder does a good job but doesn't know much about type; so I set the type for him and selected light tan cloth. Later

another package came from Amarillo and he used the dark cloth because he had no more of the other. These went to Mullin I think. I was just a go-between."

— Carl Hertzog to Lee Milazzo,
August 12, 1973.

7. *Pastores del Palo Duro.* Dallas: Southern Methodist University, 1934. Drawings and extended cover by Harold D. Bugbee. Wrappers. 16 pages. 24.6cm. × 17cm. Reprinted from *Southwest Review,* April 1934, Volume XVIV, No. 3.

8. *Charles Goodnight, Cowman and Plainsman.* Boston: Houghton Mifflin Company, 1936. Cloth. 485 pages. Illustrations by Harold D. Bugbee. Map by Thomas L. Jones. Frontispiece sketch of Colonel Goodnight. Index and bibliography. Pictorial dust-jacket. 22cm. ×14.6cm. 5,000 copies were printed in the first edition.

> *"Haley is one of the most promising writers in history that I am acquainted with. He has a very great capacity for collecting and organizing material and writes in a most delightful style. I am satisfied that a biography of Colonel Goodnight would in Haley's hands become a very illuminating study of frontier conditions in Texas, Colorado and New Mexico."*
>
> — Eugene C. Barker, March 11, 1931.

> *"Charles Goodnight, Cowman and Plainsman . . . will be received as one of the most valuable and distinctive books of its kind. . . . This book is more than a biography. It is a history of the West."*
> — L. F. Sheffy, 1936.

8b. New edition. Norman: University of Oklahoma Press, 1949. Cloth. 485 pages. 24cm. × 16cm. The physical dimensions of this edition are considerably enlarged over those of the original edition. The author's preface, "Cutting for Sign," has been expanded and revised in part. The design for the dust-jacket is completely new.

> *"Goodnight . . . summed up in himself the whole life of range and trail. Haley's book, packed with realities of incident and character, paints himself against a mighty background."*
>
> — J. Frank Dobie, in Books From
> Oklahoma About the West, 1949.

"The best biography of a cowman ever written . . . Goodnight . . . had the courage and vision to penetrate new ranges and the active intelligence to experiment with improving ranch methods. He represents the strongest aspects of American individualism. Haley's beautifully written biography, perhaps his best book, is an ample vehicle for a mighty figure, and is a classic of American biography."

> — W. S. Reese, in Six Score: the 120 Best
> Books on the Range Cattle Industry,
> 1976.

9. *Jeff Milton, A Good Man with a Gun.* Norman: University of Oklahoma Press, 1948. Cloth. 430 pages. Drawings by Harold D. Bugbee. Photographs. Map. Index. Pictorial dust-jacket. 23.8cm × 16cm. The first printing of the first edition may be identified by a typographical error in the index on page 421: the line "Greenway, John Campbell: 366, 411" is printed upside down and is not in alphabetical order. The University of Oklahoma Press advertisements on the back of the dust-jacket vary with each printing of the book.

"J. Evetts Haley tells a story with a vim and verve that lends it enchantment and fascinates the reader. Jeff Milton loved life and looked upon his every job as an adventure out of the pages of Scottish Chiefs. Put the two together and you have a perfectly matched team. The fruits of their work is a book that not only adds much to the rich lore of western history but forms a thrilling story of courage and adventure. Early in life, J. Evetts Haley, the historian, mastered the art of interviewing. This skill stood him in good stead, for Haley spent years in talking with Milton and those who knew him. From this mass of material, he sifted the chaff and produced the story of Jeff Milton.
— L. F. Sheffy, 1948.

"In February or March of 1937 I went to Tombstone to see Jeff and there by car swung around to the Northern route for my return through Flagstaff, Williams and Holbrook, to drop down from Navajo to the Z-Bar Ranch. It was still suffering the devastating effects of a terrible winter, plus bad management, but I agreed to take the job and went back to take over in the early spring. Years of intensive research and happy associates, resulted in publication in 1948 of Jeff Milton: A Good Man With a Gun by the University of Oklahoma Press.
— J. Evetts Haley, 1965. from the
"Biography of J. Evetts Haley."

10. *George W. Littlefield, Texan.* Norman: University of Oklahoma Press, 1943. Copyright 1943 by the Trustees of

the Littlefield Fund of Southern History. Cloth. 287 pages. Drawings by Harold D. Bugbee. Index. Dust-jacket. 21.6cm × 15cm.

> "In portraying the life and times of George W. Littlefield the author, J. Evetts Haley, has again proven his competence as a biographer . . . There is a human, convincing quality to this story which may be attributed to the author's own intimate knowledge of the cattle business, his familiarity with the climate and physical features of the region involved, his feeling for the land, and his ability as a raconteur. . . . His prose is vigorous, graphic, often picturesque."
>
> — C. Stanley Banks, Southwestern
> Historical Quarterly, April 1944.

10c.   Second printing, 1972. The book itself remains unchanged but yellow has been substituted for tan on the dust-jacket and copy on the jacket has been revised and partially updated.

10d.   Second printing, 1972, in stiff paper wrappers, featuring a pen and ink sketch of Littlefield by Bugbee. 21cm × 14.2cm. Issued in 1974.

11.   *Charles Schreiner, General Merchandise: The Story of a Country Store.* Austin: Texas State Historical Association, 1944. Cloth. 73 pages. Illustrated by Harold D. Bugbee, including frontispiece sketch of Captain Schreiner. Pictorial dust-jacket. Typography and design by Carl Hertzog. 23.8cm. × 16cm. 2,500 copies of this edition were printed.

11b.   "Private Edition." A special edition of 15 copies, printed on deckle-edge paper, and bound in leather were prepared for the Schreiner family, the author, and the printer.

11c.   The second edition. Kerrville: Charles Schreiner Company, 1969. This edition was reprinted by permission of the Texas State Historical Association to commemorate the centennial year of the Schreiner Company. A new foreword, "A Century of Change in a Land That Stays the Same,"

has been added by the author and slight altera-
tions have been made by the typographer.

12. *The University of Texas and The Issue.* Amarillo: Miller
Printing Company, no date (1945). Wrappers. 32 pages.
21.4cm. × 14.6 cm.

13. *Some Southwestern Trails.* San Angelo: *San Angelo
Standard-Times,* 1948. Pictorial wrappers with extended
edges. 30 pages, unnumbered. Designed and printed by
Carl Hertzog. Illustrations by Harold D. Bugbee. Cover
by Tom Lea. 22cm. × 28cm. There were 970 copies
bound in paper covers and distributed as Christmas
greetings by the publisher of the newspaper, Houston
Harte.

In addition to J. Evetts Haley, others who contributed
brief essays on outstanding trails of the West were: H.
Bailey Carroll, John L. McCarty, Jack Potter, Floyd
Streeter, Stanley Vestal, and LeRoy Hafen.

13b. Same printing with an additional 30 copies bound
in fabrikoid.

13c. The "El Paso Edition." El Paso: Carl Hertzog,
1948. Cloth. 30 pages, unnumbered. The edition
was limited to 750 copies. The title page of 75 copies was illustrated by Tom Lea with the skulls of a
horse, a buffalo, and a steer. A few of the copies
were issued with both the standard Bugbee title
page and the Lea title page bound in.

13d. The "El Paso Edition." As above, but consisting of
50 copies, specially bound in chocolate colored
cloth and issued in handmade slipcases with a
paper label.

13e. The "Special Edition." In 1949, twenty of the
copies originally bound in paper covers were
bound in Hereford Red "Homespun" and boxed as
a companion piece to *Heraldry of the Range.* (see
note under title entry.)

14. *A Bit of Bragging About a Cow*. Amarillo: George Autry, March 1948. Wrappers. 8 pages. Drawings by Harold D. Bugbee. 20cm. × 14cm.

15. *A Cowboy on Credit, or The Poppin' Off of a Panhandle Puncher to His Banker Friend*. El Paso: Carl Hertzog, 1948. Wrappers. 8 pages. 16cm. × 9cm.

16. *The Heraldry of the Range, Some Southwestern Brands*. Canyon: Panhandle-Plains Historical Society, 1949. Bound in Hereford Red "Homespun." 35 pages. Illustrated by Harold D. Bugbee. Designed and produced by Carl Hertzog. Eight facsimiles from old brand books. The fore-edges are deckle edge. 28.4cm. × 21.6cm.

   16b. Copies of the first printing were bound in stiff paper wrappers with extended edges.

   16c. The "Special Edition." Limited to twenty copies signed by Haley, Hertzog and Bugbee. Twenty copies of *Some Southwestern Trails* were specially bound to match as a companion piece to this issue of *Heraldry of the Range*, and the two volumes boxed in a slipcase covered in the same material.

17. *A Day With Dan Casement*. Kansas City: Reprinted from *The American Hereford Journal*, September 1, 1949. Wrappers. 7 pages. 22.8cm. × 15cm. 100 copies only were printed; half of the edition went to the author, and half going to Don R. Ornduff, editor of the *Journal*, who was instrumental in the production of this discursive memoir.

   "Evetts Haley . . . is one who measures up fully to my conception of a complete man. Notably contributing to this concept is his facility of expression in the written word. He has enriched our literature by valuable biographies of great men of the West who walked the earth in simpleness and gentleness and honor and clean mirth, though often enforcing, mayhap, with blazing six-guns, the righteous moral code of the frontier. Words to express my extravagant admiration for this, his gift, fail me unless I fall back on the encomium I once — to my suprise and his confusion — impulsively bestowed upon him: 'You write like a bitch

wolf.' The products of his pen reflect his sound common sense, his fine appreciation and deep understanding of human nature."
                                        —Mr. Dan D. Casement, May 11, 1951.

18. *The Great Comanche War Trail.* Canyon: Panhandle-Plains Historical Society, 1950. Wrappers. 11 pages. Illustrations and cover drawings by Harold D. Bugbee. Reprinted from *The Panhandle-Plains Historical Review*, Vol. XXIII, 1950. 22.6cm. × 15.4cm.

A brief sketch of this trail appeared in *Some Southwestern Trails* in 1948. This more extended account is a chapter from the author's then forthcoming book on Fort Concho, and was reprinted through the courtesy of Houston Harte and the *San Angelo Standard-Times.*

19. *John Bouldin's First Christmas on the Plains.* Amarillo: George Autry, 1950. Pictorial wrappers, with extended edges. 12 pages. Drawings and cover illustration by Harold D. Bugbee. 32cm. × 24cm. Privately printed for the author and distributed as a Christmas greeting.

> *"In the Fall of 1950, my friend George Autry, since deceased, a good Amarillo printer and a man motivated by deep sentiment in all such matters and especially those pertaining to the West, suggested that he, Harold Bugbee and I do a Christmas story. The first result of his suggestion was our collaboration upon what I called* John Bouldin's First Christmas On The Plains."
>   *— J.E.H. To Robert Wilson,*
>   *Dallas, January 14, 1969.*

20. *Water and Power.* Canyon: J. Evetts Haley, 1951. Wrappers. 11 pages. 15.2cm. × 8.8 cm.

21. *Then Came Christmas for Mildred Taitt.* Amarillo: George Autry, 1951. Pictorial wrappers. 12 pages (unnumbered). Drawings and cover sketch by Harold D. Bugbee. 32cm. × 24cm. Privately printed for the author and distributed as a Christmas greeting.

> *"The reception [to* John Bouldin's First Christmas on the Plains] *was good and George was enthusiastic about our continuing the idea. It was then that I came up with the thought of elaborating the story of Mildred Taitt's first Christmas in the desert along the Arizona-New Mexico border. The basic material had been collected and a little of it had been*

used in my book Jeff Milton: A Good Man With A Gun [*Norman, 1948, pp. 368-373*]. *Therefore, for the second of the series of our Christmas stories, I wrote* Then Came Christmas for Mildred Taitt *which was published by Autry.*

— *J.E.H. to Robert Wilson,*
January 14, 1969.

22. *Life on the Texas Range.* Austin: University of Texas Press, 1952. Cloth. 112 pages. Photographs by Erwin E. Smith, with text by J. Evetts Haley. Photographic frontispiece and endpapers. The slipcase is illustrated with a photograph on the upper cover. 31cm. × 23.2cm.

> *"Evetts Haley's splendid tribute . . . will perpetuate Erwin Smith's memory as an honest and skillful chronicler of life on the cattle range. Both the text and the photographic captions are rendered in pungent Haleyan style, which is characterized by a poetic prose strongly flavored with smoke from the branding fires."*
>
> — *William Curry Holden, 1952.*

  22b. Reprint edition. University of Texas Press, 1973. This edition is bound in an uninspired tan vinyl which lacks the beauty of the original edition. The dust-jacket is entirely covered by the photograph used on the slipcase of the 1952 edition.

23. *Fort Concho and the Texas Frontier.* San Angelo: *San Angelo Standard-Times*, 1952. Copyright by Houston Harte. Cloth. 352 pages. Illustrated with 37 drawings by Harold D. Bugbee; maps and plates by J. Cisneros; end papers decorated with drawings of Fort Concho from the National Archives, Washington, D.C. Index. Designed and produced by Carl Hertzog. Pictorial dust-jacket. 23.5cm. × 16cm.

  23b. The "San Angelo Edition." This edition is distinguished from the trade edition by gold lettering on the covers instead of black. The edition is limited to 185 signed copies. Each volume is numbered and signed by Carl Hertzog on the colophon page. The slipcase is also numbered on the label. Dust-jacket.

In 1952, *Fort Concho* won the Summerfield Roberts

Award given by the Sons of the Texas Republic, as the best book of the year on the frontier history of Texas.

24. *And So It Must Be . . . at Christmas . . . on the Range of Grass!* Amarillo: George Autry, 1952. Pictorial wrappers, with extended edges. 8 pages (unnumbered). Drawings and cover illustration by Harold D. Bugbee. 32cm. × 24cm. Privately printed for the author and distributed as a Christmas greeting.

25. *Christmas at the Hancock House.* Amarillo: George Autry, 1953, Pictorial wrappers, with extended edges. 8 pages. Drawings and cover illustration by Harold B. Bugbee. 32cm. × 24 cm. Privately printed for the author and distributed as a Christmas greeting.

26. *Story of the Shamrock.* Amarillo: The Shamrock Oil and Gas Corporation, 1954. Wrappers. 78 pages. Illustrations by Moranz. 26.4cm × 18cm. A business history of the first twenty-five years of the Shamrock Oil and Gas Corp.

    26b. A portion of the edition was issued in wrappers with extended edges, tied with green leather at the spine and enclosed in a cardboard slipcase.

27. *Those Who Came Before Us . . . Caught for All Time by the Brush of Harold D. Bugbee.* Amarillo: George Autry, 1955. Pictorial wrappers, with extended edges. 8 pages (unnumbered). Illustrations and cover sketch by Harold D. Bugbee. 32cm. × 24cm. The pamphlet contains two articles:

"Harold D. Bugbee, Western Artist" by J. Evetts Haley.
"The Indian Murals in the Panhandle-Plains Historical Museum" by Harold D. Bugbee.

28. *What the Teachers Think of Education. A Survey of Faculty Opinion at Texas Technological College, Lubbock, Texas.* Lubbock: The C. E. Maedgen Foundation, 1955. Wrappers. 20 pages. 20.4cm. × 12.4cm.

"The second step, and probably the most significant at the time, was the establishment of an Institute of Americanism and the appointment of J. Evetts Haley as director of the Institute. Haley, Spearman rancher-historian-Jeffersonian Democrat-individualist, will head the Institute founded by the Charles Ernest Maedgen, Sr., Foundation to promote and teach the American way of life.

"According to the Foundation's requirements, Haley will teach and emphasize the principles of free enterprise and those practices which have made America great.

"This move could be hidden in abstract generalities, but it is believed that Texas Tech has started a trend in education, adding to the classroom instruction in government, economics, history, and education, the principles of Americanism. Other schools could pick up the trend and perhaps 're-educate' the American public away from the 'give-away' system now in force."

— West Texas Today,
August 1952.

29. *When the Stagecoach Ruled the Road.* Wichita: McCormick-Armstrong Co., n.d. (1957). Pictorial wrappers, cover sketch by Bill Nye. Profusely illustrated, plus photos and maps. 21cm. × 27.6cm.

30. *Focus on the Frontier.* Amarillo: The Shamrock Oil and Gas Corporation, 1957. Leatherette. 48 pages. Photos. Typography by Carl Hertzog. 15.8cm. × 23.4cm. This edition resembles an old-fashioned photograph album.

   30b. A portion of the first edition was bound in stiff paper wrappers with extended edges. There were several trial bindings: silver ink on rose cover stock; gold ink on faded pink stock; silver on deep orange; gold on green; and silver on green.

31. *Ode to Nita by Her Husband.* (Cover title: *Nita Stewart Haley*). Canyon: Carl Hertzog for J. Evetts Haley, 1958. Private edition limited to 100 copies, none of which were for sale. 15 pages. Bound in half white and gray cloth; gold lettering on spine and upper cover. Fore-edge is deckle edge. Frontispiece photograph of Mr. and Mrs. Haley at their JH Ranch. 24.6cm. × 15.8cm. The rarest

of all Haley books, reserved for presentation to family members and intimate friends of the Haley family.

32. *Earle P. Halliburton, Genius with Cement.* Duncan Oklahoma, 1959. Copyright 1959 by J. Evetts Haley. Designed and produced by Carl Hertzog, El Paso. Pictorial cloth. 48 pages. Photographs. 16cm. × 23.4cm. 2,000 copies bound in cloth were printed for the Halliburton Oil Well Cementing Company.

  32b. Eight thousand copies were bound in stiff pictorial wrappers with extended edges for distribution by the Halliburton Company.

33. *F. Reaugh, Man and Artist.* El Paso: Carl Hertzog, 1960. Copyright 1960 by J. Evetts Haley. Published by the Shamrock Oil and Gas Corporation "for those interested in cattle and fine art." Stiff pictorial wrappers with extended edges. 16 pages (unnumbered). Seven of Reaugh's pastels are reproduced in color and four in black and white. 23.8cm. × 15.4cm.

  33b. One hundred and twenty-five copies were bound in cloth.

34. *Christmas in the Palo Duro. A Repellant World — Warmed by The Spirit.* Amarillo: The Shamrock Oil and Gas Corporation, no date (1961). Wrappers. Cover pastel by F. Reaugh. Drawings by Harold D. Bugbee. Designed by Carl Hertzog. 21.8cm. × 13.2cm.

35. *Then Came Christmas for Mildred Taitt.* Amarillo: The Shamrock Oil and Gas Corporation, 1962. Cloth. 16 pages. Drawings by Harold D. Bugbee. Typography by Carl Hertzog. 22cm. × 14cm. Four hundred copies were bound in cloth.

"For some years I had been writing little sketches of frontier characters for The Shamrock, *the company publication of the Shamrock Oil and Gas Corporation in Amarillo, at times with a special little essay for Christmas. Bob Bowen of the Shamrock Corporation, under whose jurisdiction these publications were prepared and issued, having seen the original of my Christmas Sketch on Mildred Taitt, wished to use it for their own Christmas story.*

35b.   The same in pictorial wrappers, with extended edges.

35c.   The same, bound in cloth, minus the page one salutation from the Shamrock Corporation.

35d.   The same, bound in pictorial wrappers, minus the page one salutation from the Shamrock Corporation.

35e.   Variant bindings. A few copies with, and without, the Shamrock salutation were issued in brown cloth.

"Believe me, I didn't use different colors of cloth, different kinds of paper, on the same book just to confuse the bibliographers and collectors. I was so Scotch that I used up odds and ends whenever I could. Herewith Mildred Taitt with brown cover. I like the green best.
— *Carl Hertzog to C.A.R.,*
April 24, 1974.

36.   *Men of Fiber.* El Paso: Carl Hertzog, 1963. Copyright 1963 by J. Evetts Haley. Pictorial wrappers. 40 pages. Drawings by J. Cisneros. Photos. 22.6cm. × 15.2cm. This "Shamrock Edition" was reprinted from five issues of *The Shamrock*, the magazine for friends and customers of The Shamrock Oil and Gas Corporation.

"I did conceive this series of essays for The Shamrock Oil and Gas Corporation, but not as titled in this little book. The thought for the book, and its title, came much later. There were others some of which I once thought I'd get together in another volume as More Men of Fiber, but have never found the time."
— *J. Evetts Haley to Lee Milazzo,*
March 12, 1976.

36b.   The "Rawhide Edition." Seven hundred copies were printed on Curtis Colophon and bound in imitation rawhide. The dust jacket is identical to the pictorial wrappers of the "Shamrock" edition.

37.   *A Texan Looks at Lyndon, A Study in Illegitimate Power.*
Canyon: Palo Duro Press, 1964. Pictorial stiff wrappers.
256 pages. 16cm. × 11.4cm.

The first printing of the first edition can be identified by
the ultramarine ink used on the cover, the title in red
block letters; an early "working cowboy" photograph, in
black and white, appears in a one inch circle in the upper
right corner, and the sub-title and author's name in the
lower portion of the page appear printed in reverse, being
white and rather indistinct. There were 100,000 copies of
the first printing in June, 1964.

37b.   The second printing of the first edition. This
printing is basically the same as the first except
that the color of the ink on the cover is light blue
and the sub-title and the author's name are printed
in black across most of the lower half of the front
cover.

There were 500,000 copies of the second printing of the
first edition issued in July 1964.

37c.   The first printing of the second edition. In this,
and subsequent editions, black ink is used on the
cover, and the front cover has been redesigned. A
more formal picture of the author appears in the
circle in the upper right hand corner of the cover.
The title in red is printed vertically in script instead
of block letters. Sub-title and author's name are
printed in reverse upon a solid black rectangle
covering three-quarters of the page width in the
lower portion of the cover.

In the second edition, the text on page 20, lines 9
and 10 has been revised. Originally, the copy read:

". . . Biscuits Pappy O'Daniel, the flour-salesman
Governor who had apparently voted Republican
all his life. It still . . ."

Author Haley, informed that Governor O'Daniel had *not* voted Republican all his life, changed the copy for the second edition to:

". . . Biscuits Pappy O'Daniel, the flour-salesman Governor who detested Roosevelt and his works. It still . . ."

37d.   Variant printing of second edition. One of the printers who helped produce the millions of copies of *A Texan Looks at Lyndon*, evidently didn't understand the situation and was lax in proof-reading, which resulted in lines 9, 10, and 11 on page 20 appearing in this form:

"Biscuits Pappy O'Daniel, the flour-salesman Governor. Biscuits Pappy O'Daniel, Kansas-raised flour-salesman Governor who detested Roosevelt and his works. It still." — And here the paragraph ends.

37e.   The second printing of the second edition. This printing is identical in textual content to the first printing of the second edition; however, to facilitate easier handling and to stimulate sales, the width has been trimmed to standard paperback size to allow for display in racks. 16cm. × 10.8 cm.

38.   *Early Days on the Texas New-Mexico Plains.* by Bill Oden. Edited by J. Evetts Haley. Canyon: Palo Duro Press, 1965. Cloth. 69 pages. Drawings by Harold D. Bugbee. Illustrated endpapers by J. Cisneros. Photo frontispiece. Photos. Designed and printed by Carl Hertzog. Lettering on spine and upper cover stamped in gold. 750 copies printed. 23.8cm. × 15.6cm.

> *"Although no credit has been given, the longhorn skull on the cover was drawn by Tom Lea."*
>
>   — *Harold C. Miller, El Paso, to C.A.R., March 1975.*

38b.   Variant bindings. There are four trial bindings of this volume. One is stamped in white with the full title on the spine. The remaining three copies are stamped in red, gold, and blue, with a short title: "Bill Oden." All other copies of the edition are stamped in gold with the complete title appearing on the spine.

39. *Earl Vandale on the Trail of Texas Books.* Canyon: Palo Duro Press, 1965. Cloth. 44 pages. Illustrated. Photo frontispiece. Designed and printed by Carl Hertzog. Deckle edges. 24.2cm. × 16cm. 500 copies printed.

40. *Albert Pike's Journeys in the Prairie, 1831-1832.* by Albert Pike. Introduction and notes by J. Evetts Haley. Canyon: The Panhandle-Plains Historical Society, 1969. Cloth. 91 pages. Frontispiece sketch by Olive Vandruff Bugbee. Binding designed by Carl Hertzog. "Albert Pike, Man and Author," by J. Evetts Haley appears on pages 1-15. 23cm. × 15.4 cm.

"I do not recall now how many were done in cloth. I dashed off this idea and had them done — possibly one hundred, by and for myself. Carl Hertzog probably did this cover type, as I had the work done by Shermer, in El Paso."

— *J. Evetts Haley to Lee Milazzo,*
March 12, 1976.

41. *The Strange Story of Wayne Brazel.* by Robert N. Mullin. Canyon: Palo Duro Press, 1969. 36 pages. Wrappers. Reprinted from the *Panhandle-Plains Historical Review,* Vol. XLII, 1969, with the addition of "An Introduction to Bob Mullin: Adventurer in History," by J. Evetts Haley. 22cm. × 14.4cm. Cover by J. Cisneros. Photo illustrations.

"Evetts Haley did a remarkable, almost unbelievable, job on the introduction. Before he had written a word — and I had no idea what he intended to put down — we visited in my living room in South Laguna. We talked casually, informally, for about three hours. He'd ask a question now and then. I'd reminisce about my experiences and growing up in and around El Paso. Evetts listened but never took notes or wrote while we talked. Later, when I received the fifty copies of the little book that Carl Hertzog sent to me, I marveled at the accuracy

and attention to detail Evetts had used in putting down so many of the facts I had given him. . . ."

— Robert N. Mullin to C.A.R.,
May 7, 1976.

41b. Hard cover edition. Fifty copies were bound in fine quality imitation brown leather. There is no indication that Haley edited the Mullin article. No place of publication, date, or publisher appears. Nothing identifies it as a reprint. The additional introduction by Haley which did not accompany the article in the *Panhandle Plains Historical Review* is here included. 23cm. × 15.8cm.

42. *The Flamboyant Judge, James D. Hamlin.* A Biography as Told to J. Evetts Haley and Wm. Curry Holden. Canyon: The Palo Duro Press, 1972. Cloth. 312 pages. Illustrated. Index. Dust jacket. Design and typography by Carl Hertzog and Ed Davis. Printing done by Guynes Printing Company at El Paso. Trade edition bound in half orange and green cloth. The upper cover bears a facsimile of the bronze portrait of Judge Hamlin by Glenna Goodacre, lettered directly in black. Lettering on spine in black. Frontispiece sketch of Judge Hamlin by Datus Myres. 23.4cm. × 16.5cm.

"Birth of the Book," by William Curry Holden appears on pages xi-xiii.

"Personal Reflections on Judge Hamlin," by J. Evetts Haley appears on pages xv-xxiii.

"Plea for a Fallen Woman," by Temple Houston appears in the appendix on pages 301-302.

42b. The "Bronze Limited Edition." This edition is limited to 146 numbered and boxed copies signed by J. Evetts Haley and W. C. Holden. The tail and fore-edge leaves are deckle edge. The edition is bound in half-leather and yellow cloth with lettering on the spine in gold. A bronze medallion of Judge Hamlin by Glenna Goodacre, cast by Forrest Fenn of Santa Fe, New Mexico, is inset into the upper cover. Each medallion is numbered to correspond to the number of the volume. A dust jacket is included. The volume is slightly larger than the trade edition, measuring 24.4cm. × 17cm. The slipcase is covered in the same green cloth used on the trade edition binding.

"Some note of the book's origins is necessary. In 1945, Haley and Holden recorded twenty-two hours of conversation with the aging Hamlin, and then in 1946, Hamlin dictated over two hundred pages of information to a stenographer. After the prescribed waiting period, Holden integrated the material from the two sources into manuscript form, and Haley edited, annotated, and footnoted the draft into its present form. The result is a magnificent example of how oral history can capture an individual for history when more traditional methods fail."
— *Lee C. Milazzo, from his book review in* Southwest Review, *Summer 1973.*

42c.   The "Special Limited Edition." This edition is limited to ten numbered and boxed copies, bound in full leather, and signed by J. Evetts Haley and W. C. Holden. The edition is "exclusively for R. H. Fulton." Each volume has the Goodacre/Fenn medallion of Judge Hamlin inset into the upper cover and an original watercolor by Dick Cheatham is tipped in.

42d.   The "Silver Limited Edition." This edition is limited to four numbered copies, bound in full leather, signed by J. Evetts Haley and W. C. Holden, and boxed. The Goodacre/Fenn medallion of Judge Hamlin, cast in silver, is inset into the upper cover. The four copies in this edition were specially bound for Mr. Haley, Mr. Holden, Carl Hertzog, and Forrest Fenn.

Neither the "Special" nor the "Silver" editions were by definition privately printed, but in view of the small limitation and exclusivity of distribution, they must be considered to have been produced and bound for private circulation only, and were not intended for sale to the public.

146

43. *Robbing Banks Was My Business, The Story of J. Harvey Bailey, America's Most Successful Bank Robber.* Canyon: Palo Duro Press, 1973. 210 pages. Decorated cloth with lettering in black. Design by Carl Hertzog. Blue endpapers. Illustrations by Theda Rhea. Photos. Index. Pictorial dust-jacket with color portrait of Bailey. 18.5cm. × 12.4cm.

Carl Hertzog contributed an interesting observation on the production of the book: "When getting ready for the bookbinder I always put the author's name first (top of spine) because libraries prefer this in shelving and cataloguing. So — I came up with *Haley: Robbing Banks Was My Business.* But I couldn't let that go and got Harvey Bailey in there. But at first, it was a good joke!

— Carl Hertzog to C.A.R.,
March 24, 1974.

43b. The "Paperback Edition." An edition was bound in pictorial wrappers, the design of which is the same as that used for the dust jacket of the trade edition.

43c. The "Special Edition." Two hundred copies were specially bound, numbered, and signed by Haley and Bailey. The decorated cloth is lettered in gold. The color portrait by Theda Rhea has been pasted in facing the title page. Each volume is issued in a slipcase, with a dust jacket.

43d. The "Bronze Limited Edition." A rectangular bronze sculpture portrait executed by Glenna Goodacre is inset in the upper cover. The plaque, depicting Bailey in profile against prison bars, measures 7.8cm. × 6.2cm. Twenty copies were bound in brown leather and boxed in green cloth slipcases in this personal edition for J. Evetts Haley, Dr. Jerry D. Williams, and Arrowsmith-Fenn Galleries of Santa Fe. Each copy is numbered and autographed by Haley, Bailey, Goodacre and Rhea. The sheets were printed in

1973 and the binding was accomplished in 1975.

44. *Rough Times — Tough Fiber. A Fragmentary Family Chronicle.* Canyon: Palo Duro Press, 1976. Cloth. Design and typography by Carl Hertzog. 232 pages. Photographs. Title page drawing by Joe Beeler. 23cm. × 15.5cm.

    44b. The "Midland Edition." A limited edition of 150 copies were specially bound in half leather, numbered, slipcased, and autographed by the author, J. Evetts Haley Jr., and J. Evetts Haley, III.

45. *The Alamo Mission Bell.* Austin: The Encino Press for the Nita Stewart Haley Memorial Library, Midland. Cloth. 30 pages. Drawings by E.M. "Buck" Schiwetz. 26cm. × 18cm. 1,000 copies printed in this edition.

    45b. 5,000 copies were issued bound in stiff paper wrappers, illustrated with the drawing "A Visit to the Alamo," by Schiwetz. 25.4 cm. × 17.8cm.

    45c. Two hundred and fifty copies were specially bound in half calf, slipcased, and signed by the author. The slipcase is covered with a non-durable binding paper.

    45d. The "Bell Limited Edition."

        "The sculptor, Melvin C. Warren, executed eighty-five bronze copies of the Alamo bell, two-thirds the size of the original. These were mounted on a handsome slab of walnut with a drawer containing a full leather bound copy of The Alamo Bell *printed on handmade paper. These were done for the purpose of paying off the $125,000 indebtedness incurred through purchase of the bell, and for the benefit of the Nita Stewart Haley Memorial Library."*
                — Mrs. Nancy R. McKinley,
                Midland, Texas, June 27, 1975.

The publication price of the copies in this edition was $2,500.

Each title page of the 6,340 copies of *The Alamo*

Mission Bell bears the line "Bronze executed by Melvin C. Warren." This credit pertains solely to the eight-five copies of the "Bell Limited Edition." For the sake of accuracy and clarity, the credit line should have been deleted from the title pages of those copies which were part of the other editions. A small oversight by the editor of an otherwise beautifully designed volume.

45e. The "Midland Edition." Five copies were specially bound in leather and boxed in a slip-case covered with marbled paper. Each originator in the Bell project received a copy: Ray Whiteside, Don Bradshaw, Ray Stewart, John Haley, and Evetts Haley, Jr.

46. *Ranges of Grass and the Men on Horseback.* El Paso: Crawford Penick, Inc., 1976. 4 pages. Illustration by Harold D. Bugbee. Cover design by William D. Wittliff. 28cm. × 22.5cm. The front cover features a Charles M. Russell ink drawing done for use as an illustration for the Program of the 40th Annual Convention of the Montana Stockgrowers Association in 1925. The article by Haley under the cover is "Betty and Her Books," reprinted from Betty Smedley's *Catalogue No. 11* issued in Austin in 1976.

SECTION B

~

ARTICLES AND MISCELLANY

Arranged Alphabetically

ARTICLES IN ANNUALS AND PERIODICALS

47. "Adventurous Lens of Erwin Smith," *The Shamrock*, Fall 1956. Pp. 3-8. Photos by Erwin E. Smith.

48. "All in a Day's Work," *The Shamrock*, Summer 1956. Pp. 2-8. Photos by Erwin E. Smith.

49. "— And Then Came Barbed Wire To Change History's Course," *The Cattleman*, March 1927, Vol. XIII, No. 10. Pp. 78-83.

50. "John Armstrong, Texas Ranger," *The Shamrock*, Fall 1963. Pp. 2-6, 15. Photos.

51. "Back-trailin' with the Old Timers," *The Cattleman*, March 1933, Vol. XIX, No. 10. Pp. 11,13,15. Illustrations by Harold D. Bugbee. Photo.

52. "Back Trailing with the Old Timers. Bob Beverly — a Living Testimonial to the Encouraging Truth That Rugged Character Is Not Eroded by Time," *The Cattleman*, May 1944, Vol. XXX, No. 12. Pp. 13-14.

53. "John R. Baylor, Irrepressible Rebel," *The Shamrock*, Fall 1961. Pp. 8-11,15. Photos.

54. "The Bell Ranch," *The Shamrock*, November 1947. Pp. 10-11. Drawing by H. D. Bugbee. Photos.

55. "Ab Blocker, Trail Boss," *The Shamrock*, Summer 1958. Pp. 11-14. Drawings by Harold D. Bugbee.

56. "Bob Beverly, Cowboy Sheriff," *The Shamrock*, Summer 1963. Pp. 2-6. Photos.

57. "John Bouldin's first Christmas on the Plains," *The Shamrock*, Christmas 1958. Pp. 8-11. Drawings by Harold D. Bugbee.

58. "Buffalo Hunter," *The Shamrock*, Fall 1957. Pp. 10-14. Drawings by H. D. Bugbee. Photos by L. A. Huffman.

59. "Dick Bussell, Buffalo Hunter," *Ranch Romances*, December 14, 1934. Drawing by H. D. Bugbee.

60. "The Butterfield Trail," *The Cementer*, March-April 1964. Pp. 18-19. Illustration by H. D. Bugbee.

61. "The Cattleman Cover, Longhorns In the Buffalo Trail — Harold D. Bugbee," *The Cattleman*, October 1946, Vol. XXXIII, No. 5, P. 9.

62. "Christmas at the Hancock House," *The Shamrock*, Christmas 1959. Pp. 8-11. Drawings by Harold D. Bugbee. Photos.

63. "Christmas on The Range," *The Shamrock*, Nov.-Dec. 1955. Pp. 2-3. Drawing by Harold D. Bugbee.

64. "The Comanchero Trade," *Southwestern Historical Quarterly*, January 1935, Vol. XXXVIII, No. 3. Pp. 157-176.

65. "Committee Visits King Ranch," *The Cattleman*, April 1931. Pp. 26-28.

66. "Jim Cook, On the Frontiers of Fantasy," *The Shamrock*, Spring 1964. Pp. 4-7. Illustrated.

67. "Cowboy Sheriff," *Texas Permian Historical Annual*, December 1963, Vol. III, No. 1. Pp. 18-22.

68. "Cowboys' Part in Plains History Was Vital," *The Cattleman*, December 1925, Vol. XII, No. 7. Pp. 43-47.

69. "Cowboys Went on a Strike," *The Cattleman*, March 1931. Pp. 58.

70. "Cow Business and Monkey Business," *Saturday Evening Post*, December 8, 1934. Pp. 26,28-29,94,96. Photos.

71. "The Cows are in the Cotton Patch," *West Texas Today*, November 1933. Pp. 10, 20.

72. "The Cross L Brand," *The Shamrock*, April 1948. Pp. 9-10. Drawing by Harold D. Bugbee.

73. "A Day With Dan Casement," *American Hereford Journal*, September 1, 1949. Pp. 24-25, 28-29, 32, 152. Photos.

74. "General Grenville M. Dodge, Builder of Railroads," *The Shamrock*, Spring 1961. Pp. 9-11. Photos.

75. "Driving A Trail Herd," *Southwest Review*, July 1933, Vol. XVIII, No. 4. Pp. 383-403.

76. "Jim East, Trail Hand and Cowboy," *Panhandle-Plains Historical Review*, 1931, Vol. 4. Pp. 39-61.

77. "Ben Ficklin, Pioneer Mail Man," *The Shamrock*, Spring 1959. Pp. 8-12. Drawings by H. D. Bugbee. Photo.

78. "Focus on the Frontier," *The Shamrock*, Sept.-Oct. 1955. Pp. 2-8. Photos by L. A. Huffman.

79. "A Glamorous Past Walks With Him. Judge Hamlin, XIT Ranch's 'South Ender,' is More Than a Man: He is History at Its Happiest," *West Texas Today*, May 1934. Pp. 18,62-63.

80. "Charles Goodnight's Indian Recollections," *Frontier Times*, December 1928, Vol. 6, No. 3. Pp. 135-143.

81. "Charles Goodnight's Indian Recollections," *Panhandle-Plains Historical Review*, 1928, Vol. I, No. 1. Pp. 3-29.

82. "Charles Goodnight, Pioneer," *Panhandle-Plains Historical Review*, 1930, Vol. III. Pp. 7-17.

83. "Charles Goodnight: Pioneer Cattleman," *Persimmon Hill*, A Quarterly of the West. Summer 1970, Vol. 1, No. 1. Pp. 9-12.

84. "The Goodnight Trail," *The Shamrock*, August 1946.

85. "The Goodnight Trail, *Panhandle-Plains Historical Review*, 1946, Vol. XIX. Illustrated by H. D. Bugbee.

86. "Grass Fires of the Southern Plains," *West Texas Historical Association Year Book*, June 1929, Vol. V. Pp. 23-42.

87. "The Grass Lease Fight and Attempted Impeachment of the First Panhandle Judge," *Southwestern Historical Quarterly*, July 1934, Vol. XXXVIII, No. 1. Pp. 1-27.

88. "The Great Comanche War Trail," *Panhandle-Plains Historical Review*, 1950, Vol. XXIII. Pp. 11-21.

89. "The Great Comanche War Trail," *The Cementer,* March-April 1964. Pp. 34-35. Drawings by H. D. Bugbee.

90. "The Great Plains: A New Plan for History Writing," *Frontier Times,* March 1932, Vol. 9, No. 6. Pp. 287-288.

91. "The Great Plains History Collection," *The Alcalde,* June 1933, Vol. XXI, No. 10. Pp. 201-202. Illus.

92. "The Great Resoluter — Heads the Largest Chamber of Commerce In The World; Its in Texas and New Mexico," *The Caduceus of Kappa Sigma,* October 1934. Pp. 26-31. Photo.

93. "Bill Greene of Cananea Copper," *The Shamrock,* Summer 1962. Pp. 4-7. Photos.

94. "Mrs. John A. Haley (1867-1943)," *The Southwestern Historical Quarterly,* April 1944, Vol. XLVII, No. 4. Pp. 397-399.

95. "Erle P. Halliburton, Cementer," *The Shamrock,* Summer 1964. Pp. 4-6. Photos.

96. "The Heraldry of the Range, Some Southwestern Brands," *The Shamrock,* September 1947. Pp. 10-11. Drawing by Harold D. Bugbee.

97. "The Heraldry of the Range, Some Southwestern Brands," *The Cementer,* March-April 1964, Vol. 20, No. 2. Pp. 8-9. Drawing by H. D. Bugbee.

98. "The Hide Hunt," *The Shamrock,* February 1949.

99. "Historic Saddle is Saved," *The Cattleman,* January 1927, Vol. XIII, No. 8. P. 30. Photo.

100. "The Horses of the Conquest: An Appreciation of Cunninghame Graham's Work," *The Cattleman,* December 1949. Vol. XXXVI, No. 7. Pp. 60-62.

101. "Horses," *The Cattleman*, September 1940, Vol. XXXVI, No. 4. P. 42.

102. "Horse Thieves," *Southwest Review*, Spring 1930, Vol. XV, No. 3. Pp. 317-332.

103. "Huffman and the Montana Cow Country," *The Shamrock*, Nov.-Dec. 1955. Pp. 4-15. Photos.

104. "Indian Ways and Times," *The Shamrock*, January 1949.

105. "The JA Ranch," *The Shamrock*, January 1948. Pp. 8-10. Photos. Drawing by H. D. Bugbee.

106. "The JJ Brand," *The Shamrock*, May 1948. Pp. 7-8. Photos. Drawing by Harold D. Bugbee.

107. "Ray C. Johnson, Gentleman and Lawyer," *The Shamrock*, Fall 1959. Pp. 6-7. Portrait of Mr. Johnson by Moranz.

108. "Dad Joiner, Wildcatter," *The Shamrock*, Fall 1962. Pp. 10-13. Photos.

109. "L'Archeveque, the Outlaw," *The Shamrock*, Fall 1958. Pp. 12-15. Photos. Drawing by H. D. Bugbee.

110. "The Last Great Chief," *The Shamrock*, Spring 1957. Pp. 14-19. Photos. Drawing by H. D. Bugbee.

111. "Letter to Bailey," *Southwestern Historical Quarterly*, October 1944, Vol. XLVIII, No. 2. Pp. 298-300.

112. "Letter to Walter P.," *Southwestern Historical Quarterly*, July 1944, Vol. XLVIII, No. 1. Pp. 112-116.

113. "Longhorn, Lasso and Latigo," *Nature Magazine*, December 1930, Vol. XVI, No. 6. Pp. 371-374,386. Photos.

114. "R. S. Mackenzie, Indian Fighter," *The Shamrock*, Spring 1958. Pp. 8-11. Photos. Drawings by Harold D. Bugbee.

115. "The Making of a Scout," *True West*, May-June 1966, Vol. 13, No. 5. Pp. 6-10, 66-67. Photos.

116. "Marcy — Explorer," *The Shamrock*, Summer 1957. Pp. 10-14. Drawings by H. D. Bugbee.

117. "The Marcy Trail," *The Cementer*, March-April 1964. Pp. 24-25. Drawing by H. D. Bugbee.

118. "The Matador Brand," *The Shamrock*, March 1948. Pp. 9-10. Photos. Drawing by Harold D. Bugbee.

119. "Dave McCormick, Pioneer," *Ranch Romances*, July 14, 1934, Vol. LXXIV, No. 2. Pp. 228-233. Drawings by Harold D. Bugbee.

120. "Mustangs — Wild Horses of the Plains," *The Shamrock*, April 1949.

121. "News Items," *Southwestern Historical Quarterly*, Vol. XXXVI, No. 3, January 1933. Pp. 247-248.

122. "News Notes," *Southwestern Historical Quarterly*, Vol. XXXVII, No. 3, January 1934. Pp. 235-236.

123. "The 101 Brand," *The Shamrock*, February 1948. Pp. 10-11. Photos. Drawing by Harold D. Bugbee.

124. "The Panhandle of the Old Cowman," *The Cattleman*, February 1931, Vol 17, No. 9. Pp. 13-15,17-19,21. Illustrated.

125. "Pastores del Palo Duro," *Southwest Review*, April 1934, Vo. XVIV, No. 3. Pp. 279-294. Drawings by Harold D. Bugbee.

126. "Andrew Jackson Potter, Fighting Parson," *The Shamrock*, Summer 1961. Pp. 8-11. Photos.

127. "Portraits of the West. Harold Bugbee, Cowboy Artist, Paints the Texas Cow Camp and Trail," *The Alcalde*,

Jan.-Feb. 1930, Vol. XVIII, No. 5. Pp. 187-190. Drawings by Harold D. Bugbee.

128. "The Rath Trail," *The Shamrock*, February 1947.

129. "The Rath Trail," *Panhandle-Plains Historical Review*, 1946, Vol. XIX. Drawings by Harold D. Bugbee.

130. "F. Reaugh, Man and Artist," *The Shamrock*, Summer 1960. Pp. 8-12, Paintings by F. Reaugh. Photos.

131. "Report on Textbook Hearings," *Speaking of Education*, 1961, Vol. 8, No. 1. Pp. 5-6,17.

132. "Satanta, the Orator of the Plains, *The Shamrock*, Spring 1960. P. 8-11. Photos.

133. "Charles Schreiner, Pioneer Merchant," *The Shamrock*, Spring 1963. Pp. 6-9. Drawing by Harold D. Bugbee. Photos.

134. "Scouting With Goodnight," *Southwest Review*, April 1932, Vol. XVII, No. 3. Pp. 267-289. Drawings by Harold D. Bugbee.

135. "Scouting With Goodnight," *Frontier Times*, December 1932, Vol. 10, No. 3. Pp. 131-144.

136. "Charlie Siringo, Cowboy Chronicler," *The Shamrock*, Spring 1962. Pp. 5-7,15. Photos.

137. "Hank Smith, Frontier Settler," *The Shamrock*, Fall 1960. Pp. 2-5. Photos.

138. "Martha Summerhayes, Frontier Army Wife," *The Shamrock*, Summer 1959. Pp. 8-12. Photos.

139. "Texas Control of Texas Soil — Shall True Texas Traditions, or a 'Philosophy of Confusion', Make Our Politics?," *West Texas Today*, July 1936. Pp. 14-16.

140. "Texas Fever and the Winchester Quarantine," *Panhandle-Plains Historical Review,* 1935, Vol. VIII. Pp. 37-53.

141. "Texas Great Plains Country," *The Shamrock,* Spring 1956. Pp. 2-7. Photos by M. C. Ragsdale.

142. "Texian Saddles," *The Cattleman,* June 1938, Vol. 25, No. 1, Pp. 13-14. Photos.

143. "This Plainsman Comes Forth," *The Alcalde,* October 1931, Vol. XX, No. 2. Pp. 6-8. Photo.

144. "Up the Potomac Without a Paddle," *Oklahoma Farm and Ranch,* April 1964. Pp. 13-14.

145. "War on Rustlers," *Ranch Romances,* February 4, 1938, Vol. LXXVIII, No. 3. Pp. 110-117. Drawings by H. D. Bugbee.

146. "Work and Play on the Range," *The Shamrock,* Winter 1956. Pp. 13-17. Photos by Erwin Smith.

147. "The XIT Brand," *The Shamrock,* October 1947. Pp. 9-10. Drawings by Harold D. Bugbee.

148. "The XIT Brand," *Southwestern Crop and Stock,* November 1947, Vol. 1, No. 11. Pp. 7,31. Drawing by Harold D. Bugbee.

149. "The XIT Brand," *The Branding Iron,* November 20, 1947, Vol. 2, No. 4. Drawing by Harold D. Bugbee.

150. "The XIT Brand," *Souvenir Program, 13th Annual XIT Rodeo-Reunion, July 28-29-30, Dalhart, Texas.* Dalhart: Bishop Office Supply, 1949. Drawing by Harold D. Bugbee. Pp. 26-27.

151. "Yesteryear's Christmas With The Cowboys," *The Shamrock,* Christmas 1958. Pp. 2-4. Drawings by H. D. Bugbee.

152. "Young Cow Hands Become Old Timers," *The Cattleman*, March 1929, Vol. XX, No. 10. Pp. 33,35,37,39. Photos.

ARTICLES IN NEWSPAPERS

153. "Benediction of Nature." An editorial in *The Amarillo Times*, February 18, 1938.

154. "Blood on the Moon." An editorial in *The Amarillo Times*, March 26, 1938.

155. "T. S. Bugbee, Second Ranchman in the Panhandle." An article in the feature section of the *Dallas Morning News*, November 15, 1925.

156. "Commendable Theft of Stone of Scone." A column in the series "Texas Tory Talk" in *The San Angelo Standard-Times*, November 12, 1950.

157. "Complete Mobilization Not the Answer." A column of "Texas Tory Talk" in *The San Angelo Standard-Times*, December 17, 1950.

158. "Compulsory Education Versus Freedom." A Texas Tory Talk column in *The San Angelo Standard-Times*, October 22, 1950.

159. "Congressional Race In The Panhandle." The "Texas Tory Talk" column in *The San Angelo Standard-Times*, November 5, 1950.

160. "Cowboy's Part in Plains History Was Vital." *The Amarillo Daily News*, November 15, 1925.

161. "Cows In the Cotton Patch." *San Antonio Express*, October 13, 1935.

162. "Cows In the Cotton Patch." *The Chicago Sunday Tribune.* November 3, 1935.

163. "The Federal Menace To Education." *San Antonio Express*, Sunday, September 2, 1935.

164. "Federalized Education." *San Antonio Express,* October 20, 1935.

165. "The First White Woman on the Texas Plains." An article in *The Dallas Morning News,* June 28, 1925, in the Feature Section.

166. "For High Crimes and Misdemeanors." A column in the series "Texas Tory Talk" in *The San Angelo Standard-Times,* October 29, 1950.

167. "The Frontiers of Freedom." A column in *The Amarillo Times,* October 11, 1938.

168. "Gone With The Wind." An editorial in *The Amarillo Times,* April 20, 1958.

169. "Haley Discusses Old Chroniclers: Part 2." An article in the series "Cowboy Chroniclers" in *The Midland Reporter-Telegram,* September 13, 1931.

170. "Haley Discusses Old Chroniclers: Part 3." An article in the series "Cowboy Chroniclers" in *The Midland Reporter-Telegram,* September 14, 1931.

171. "Haley Discusses Old Chroniclers: Part 4." Last in the "Cowboy Chroniclers" series in *The Midland Reporter-Telegram,* September 18, 1931.

172. "The Heritage of Nature." A column in *The Amarillo Times,* September 14, 1938.

173. "The High Road To National Ruin." A column in *The Amarillo Times,* November 17, 1938.

174. "The Higher Cost of Higher Education." An editorial in *The Amarillo Times,* April 28, 1938.

175. "Incipient Revolt On The High Plains." A "Texas Tory Talk" column in *The San Angelo Standard-Times,* January 7, 1951.

176. "In Search of Unity For Our Future." A column in the "Texas Tory Talk" series in *The San Angelo Standard-Times,* December 22, 1950.

177. "It's About Time To Pull In Our Horns." One of the "Texas Tory Talk" columns in *The San Angelo Standard-Times,* February 11, 1951.

178. "Just How Much Is The Dollar Worth?" A column in the series "Texas Tory Talk" in *The San Angelo Standard-Times,* February 11, 1951.

179. "Last Honors Paid Pioneer Resident In Services Friday." *The Midland Reporter-Telegram,* January 2, 1938. This sketch of the life history of Evetts Haley's father, Hon. John A. Haley, was read at the funeral and was printed in the newspaper with permission of the Haley family.

180. "The Legislature and The University." A column in the series "Texas Tory Talk" in *The San Angelo Standard-Times,* March 25, 1951.

181. "Literature and the Law of Necessity." One of the "Texas Tory Talk" columns, *The San Angelo Standard-Times,* April 8, 1951.

182. "Little Comfort For Truman in Texas." This column is the first in the series entitled "Texas Tory Talk" which started in *The San Angelo Standard-Times,* September 3, 1950.

183. "Bishop Lucey In Defense of CIO." A column in *The Amarillo Times,* October 7, 1938.

184. "Making A Mess Of The Cotton Business." One of the "Texas Tory Talk" columns in *The San Angelo Standard-Times,* March 11, 1951.

185. "A Man May be Crazy — or Merely be Starting Toward a Big Fire." *The Prairie*, February 10, 1925.

186. "Midland Historian Fans Brands of Western Literature in Talk Here; Praises The Chroniclers." First article in the series "Cowboy Chroniclers" in *The Midland Reporter-Telegram*, September 11, 1931.

187. "More Controls Only Means Less Beef." One of the columns in the series "Texas Tory Talk" in *The San Angelo Standard-Times*, April 15, 1951.

188. "A New Deal In Culture." *San Antonio Express*, November 19, 1935.

189. "A New Deal In Culture." *The Amarillo Globe*, Sunday, November 17, 1935.

190. "On Government Boards And Economy." A column in the series "Texas Tory Talk" in *The San Angelo Standard-Times*, December 10, 1950.

191. "On Purging The Literary Pinks." From *The San Angelo Standard-Times* series "Texas Tory Talk," February 25, 1951.

192. "Our Greatest Threat Is Now Internal." A "Texas Tory Talk" in *The San Angelo Standard-Times*.

193. "Panhandle Hopeful of Future As Plans Made for Fight on Worst Dust Storm in History." *The Dallas Morning News*, April 17, 1935.

194. "The Panhandle-Plains Historical Society." *Lubbock Avalanche*, September 27, 1925.

195. "People of the Plains, Bob Smith." An article in *The Amarillo Times*, June 3, 1945.

196. "People of the Plains, Fred Scott." *The Amarillo Times*, July 15, 1945.

197. "People of the Plains, Colonel Jack Potter." *The Amarillo Times*, September 9, 1945.

198. "Possibilities of the Palo Duro." *The Amarillo Times*, November 28, 1938.

199. "Price Control: The Same Old Baloney." A column in the series "Texas Tory Talk" in *The San Angelo Standard-Times*, March 11, 1951.

200. "Primary Obligation Is To The Party." A column in the "Texas Tory Talk" series in *The San Angelo Standard-Times*, September 17, 1950.

201. "The Questionable Federal Bounty." *San Antonio Express*, Sunday, September 15, 1935.

202. "The Significance Of Texas Matadors." A "Texas Tory Talk" article in *The San Angelo Standard-Times*, April 25, 1951.

203. "The Sit-Down Addicts and The Dies Committee." An article in *The Amarillo Times*, November 18, 1938.

204. "A Sorry Substitute For Diplomacy." A column in the "Texas Tory Talk" series in *The San Angelo Standard-Times*, February 18, 1951.

205. "A State of Crisis." *The Amarillo Times*, September 13, 1938.

206. "Sunset on the Palo Duro." An editorial in *The Amarillo Times*, May 13, 1938.

207. "Texas Wildlife Federation Coming To The Plains." A column in *The Amarillo Times*, November 24, 1938.

208. "There's Something About It." *The Amarillo Times*, September 10, 1938.

209. "Time To Purge The United Nations." A column in "Texas Tory Talk" in *The San Angelo Standard-Times*, January 28, 1951.

210. "Tory Talk of Mickey, Mice, and Men." In the "Texas Tory Talk" series, *The San Angelo Standard-Times*, September 10, 1950.

211. "Traveler Finds 'A Touch of Texas' Far From Home." An article in the *Abilene Reporter-News*, March 31, 1950.

> *"I believe it was in 1950 that Evetts joined Henry in a magnificent publicity stunt by which they transported, by chartered plane, a small steer from Boys' Ranch to Hereford House (a new restaurant) in Bronxville, New York. The plane was emblazoned "A little bull goes a long way!", and made stops at major cities where they drew crowds of curious and interested people. The Hereford House had all media on hand to interview these Texas cowboys, and Evetts was on radio and in the floorshow with lots of funny stuff."*
> — *Mrs. Henry Sears, Hereford, Texas,*
> *to C.A.R., October 21, 1974.*

212. "Mr. Truman Not Really Responsible." A column in the "Texas Tory Talk" series in *The San Angelo Standard-Times*, January 14, 1951.

213. "Universal Military Training Vs. the Lessons of History." *The Amarillo Register*, June 17, 1955.

214. "Water, Water, But Not Everwhere." In the "Texas Tory Talk" series, *The San Angelo Standard-Times*, November 19, 1950.

215. "West Texas Breezes." The title of a column of observations that appeared in *The Prairie*, weekly newspaper of The West Texas State Teachers College, October 7, 14, 21 and November 4, 11, 18, 1924.

216. "When the Panhandle Was Still Young." An article in *The Dallas Morning News*, August 2, 1925.

217. "When Mr. White Goes To Washington." In the "Texas Tory Talk" series in *The San Angelo Standard-Times*, October 1, 1950.

218. "Why The Political Pot Boils in Texas." *The Amarillo Register*, July 1, 1955.

ARTICLES EDITED BY
J. EVETTS HALEY

219. Bell, James G., "A Log of the Texas-California Cattle Trail, 1854." Part I. Edited by J. Evetts Haley. *Southwestern Historical Quarterly,* January 1932, Vol. XXXV, No. 3. Pp. 208-237.

    A. ⎯⎯⎯⎯⎯⎯ Part II. *Southwestern Historical Quarterly,* April 1932, Vol. XXXV, No. 4. Pp. 290-316.

    B. ⎯⎯⎯⎯⎯⎯ Part III. *Southwestern Historical Quarterly,* July 1932, Vol. XXXVI, No. 1. Pp. 47-66.

220. Casement, Dan D., *The Address of Mr. Dan D. Casement at the Thirtieth Annual Meeting of the Panhandle-Plains Historical Society at Canyon, Texas, May 11, 1951.* Edited by J. Evetts Haley. Amarillo: George Autry and J. Evetts Haley, 1951. Wrappers. 8 pp. 23.8cm. × 15.6cm.

221. Edmondson, Alta, "E. Irving Couse — Painter of Indians." *Panhandle-Plains Historical Review,* 1969, Vol. XLII. Pp. 1-21. Illustrated with five paintings by Couse. Photos.

    A. ⎯⎯⎯⎯⎯⎯ *E. Irving Couse — Painter of Indians.* Canyon: Palo Duro Press, 1969. Reprinted from the *Panhandle-Plains Historical Review, 1969,* at Amarillo by the press of George Autry Printer. Pictorial wrappers with reproduction in color of Couse's oil painting "Repairing The Quiver." 22 pp. The edition was limited to 100 copies. 21.8cm. × 14.4cm.

222. Frame, Mrs. Rosalind Kress, "Is This the Rockefeller Blueprint designed to destroy the Reagan Movement in your state?" A political broadside edited and annotated by J. Evetts Haley; designed and printed by Carl Hertzog at El Paso. It was published by Texans for Ronald Reagan at Fort Worth, January 15, 1968. 28cm. × 21.5cm.

223. McGowan, Hon. M. M., *The Jury — Barrier to Tyranny*. Edited and annotated by J. Evetts Haley. Canyon: Texans For America, undated (1965). 6 pp. Wrappers. Designed and printed by Carl Hertzog. There were 1200 copies printed. A few were issued with additional paper covers, with extended edges. 23cm. × 15cm.

> *"Dear Judge McGowan: Margaret has sent me your essay upon the background and the vital nature of the jury system as the last safeguard of human freedom. It is the finest dissertation of its kind that I have ever read and I want to have it printed in attractive broadside form by this organization. I trust you have no objection to my doing so.*
>
> *"Acting upon this presumption, I am sending a copy of it to my friend, Carl Hertzog, one of the greatest of American printers with the hope that he can find time to take care of the typography and to convert it to the attractive form which it really deserves for general circulation.*
>
> *"If we cannot hold the line against the destruction of this, the last of our Anglo-Saxon freedoms, then we are truly a police state."*
> — *J. Evetts Haley to Judge McGowan*
> *November 23, 1965.*

224. Moon, Mrs. Ilanon, *Textbook Criteria For Young Americans*. Preface and footnotes by J. Evetts Haley. Fort Worth: Texas Committee for Education, 1960. Designed and printed by Carl Hertzog, El Paso. 8 pp. 23cm. × 10cm.

225. Moore, Ealy. "A Log of the Montana Trail as Kept by Ealy Moore." *Panhandle-Plains Historical Review*, 1932. Vol. V. Pp. 44-56.

226. _____ "A Log of the Montana Trail as Kept by Ealy Moore." Edited by J. Evetts Haley. *The Cattleman*, February 1934, Vol. XX, No. 9. Pp. 30-33.

227. Pike, Albert, "Albert Pike's Journeys in the Prairie 1831-1832." Introduction and notes by J. Evetts Haley. *Panhandle-Plains Historical Review,* 1968, Vol. XLI. Pp. 1-91.

SPEECHES: PUBLISHED AND UNPUBLISHED

228. *Americanism Without Apology.* Keynote address at the 35th Annual Convention of the West Texas Chamber of Commerce, October 20, 1952, Wichita Falls, Texas. Wrappers. 12 pp. (unnumbered). No date (1952). 21.2cm. × 9.6cm.

229. "The Eugene C. Barker Portrait, Presentation." The principal address delivered at the presentation to the University of Texas of the portrait by Robert Joy. *The Southwestern Historical Quarterly,* April 1943, Vol. XLVI, No. 3. Pp. 301-312.

   A.   A pamphlet reprinted from *The Southwestern Historical Quarterly,* April 1943. Wrappers. 27 pp. Frontispiece. 24cm. × 16cm.

230. "Board and Museum Relationships." An address to the Fall 1955 meeting of the Mountain-Plains Division of The American Association at Fort Worth. *Panhandle-Plains Historical Review,* 1956, Vol. 39. Pp. 33-43. (See also: *Some Problems of Museum Board Relationships.*)

231. "Casual Comment on Current Trends." An address before the Council of Alpha Chi, Austin, Texas, 1935. *Pro-*

*ceedings of the Fourteenth Annual Meeting of the Council
of Alpha Chi,* 1935.. Pp. 12-20.

A.   A reprint in wrappers. 8 pp. (unnumbered). No
date, (1935). 21.8cm. × 15cm.

232. "The Constitution and Its Betrayal." A speech given
before the Republican Minute Men, Tulsa, Oklahoma, on
September 30, 1965. 23 pp. Unpublished, typed
manuscript.

233. "Farewell to the Panhandle-Plains Historical Society." A
two-page, typewritten, unpublished manuscript of the
speech delivered at Canyon, 1952.

234. "Interposition and States Rights." A speech delivered at a
political rally at Amarillo, Texas, June 21, 1956. 18 pp.
Unpublished, typed manuscript.

235. "Introduction of Mr. Rarick by J. Evetts Haley." A
four-page, typed introduction delivered at Amarillo,
Texas, March 18, 1975, before a meeting of the Texas
Committee of the Constitution.

236. *The New Deal in Texas.* A radio address on the Texas
Quality Network on October 15, 1936, when Haley was
chairman of the Jeffersonian Democrats of Texas. Austin:
Jeffersonian Democrats of Texas, October 1936. Wrappers. 12 pp. 23cm. × 10.5cm.

237. "Our Constitution and Our Republic's Survival." A
speech delivered to the Freedom Club, Los Angeles, October 13, 1964. 16 pp. Unpublished, typed manuscript.

238. *Painting and Prejudice — A Comment on the Nature of
Cultivated Degeneracy.* A critical paper read to the annual dinner of the Coppini Academy of Fine Arts, San
Antonio, Texas, January, 1961. El Paso: Carl Hertzog.
Wrappers, with extended edges. No date (1961). 14 pp.
(unnumbered). There were 500 copies printed. 23.8cm. ×
15.4cm.

239. *Patriotism in Our Own "Hour of Decision."* An address presented to the Panhandle Plains Regional Meeting of the Natural Gasoline Association of America, Herring Hotel, Amarillo, Texas, November 20, 1951. Amarillo: George Autry. No date, (1951). Wrappers. 4 pp. (unnumbered). 27.8cm. × 21.4cm.

240. "The Quest for Story Material." A lecture given at the Writer's Conference held at Eastern New Mexico University, Portales, New Mexico, June 10, 1954. 25 pp. Unpublished, typed manuscript.

241. *Some Problems of Museum Board Relationships.* Canyon: J. Evetts Haley, 1956. Wrappers. 12 pp. Reprinted from *The Panhandle-Plains Historical Review,* 1956, Vol. 24, titled "Board and Museum Relationships." 22.2cm. × 14.8cm.

242. "Testimony of J. Evetts Haley." in *Report to the Members of the Texas House of Representatives of the 58th Legislature on the Dallas Textbook Hearing of May 31, 1962.* Austin: Privately printed by W. T. Dungan, Chairman of the Textbook Committee, 1962. Wrappers. Pp. 77-86. 27.4cm. × 21cm.

243. "A Texan Still Looks At Lyndon." A speech delivered at the First National Convention of the Liberty Lobby, Sheraton Park Hotel, Washington, D.C., January 6, 1967. 23 pp. Unpublished, typed manuscript.

244. "The Texas Historical Survey." A paper read by J. Evetts Haley at the Annual Meeting of the Texas State Historical Association held at Austin, Texas, April 20-21, 1934. 18 pp. Unpublished, typed manuscript. Mr. Haley was a member of the Executive Council of the Association for the term ending 1937.

245. *To the Cowboy Artists of America.* A speech delivered to The Cowboy Artists of America's Eleventh Annual Show, Phoenix, Arizona, October 23, 1976. Copyright by the Palo Duro Press, Canyon, Texas, 1976. Printed at El

Paso, Texas, by Guynes Printing Company. Wrappers, with extended edges. 8pp. Cover illustration by Joe Beeler. 23cm. × 15cm.

BOOK REVIEWS

246. Allen, Jules Verne, *Cowboy Lore. Southwestern Historical Quarterly*, Vol. XXXVII, No. 1, July 1933. P. 72.

247. Baldwin, Alec Blackwood, *Memoirs of the Late Frank D. Baldwin. Southwestern Historical Quarterly*, Vol. XXXVII, No. 1, July 1933. Pp. 70-71.

248. Boatright, Mody C., *Tall Tales of Texas Cow Camps. Southwestern Historical Quarterly*, Vol. XXXVIII, No. 3, January 1935. Pp. 230-31.

249. *Bulletin of the Sam Houston State Teachers College 1931. Southwestern Historical Quarterly*, Vol. XXXV, No. 4, April 1932. P. 336.

250. Burton, Harley True, *A History of the JA Ranch. Panhandle-Plains Historical Review*, Vol. II, 1929. Pp. 152-153.

251. Canton, Frank M., *Frontier Trails. Southwestern Historical Quarterly, Vol. XXXV, No. 4, April 1932. Pp. 331-332.*

252. Connelley, William Elsey, *Wild Bill and His Era: The Life and Adventures of James Butler Hickock. Southwestern Historical Quarterly*, Vol. XXXVIII, No. 1, July 1934. Pp. 74-75.

253. Coolidge, Dane, *Fighting Men of the West*. *Southwestern Historical Quarterly*, Vol. XXXVI, No. 1, July 1932. Pp. 75-76.

254. Cushing, Frank Hamilton, *Zuni Folk Tales*. *Southwestern Historical Quarterly*, Vol. XXXVI, No. 1, July 1932. Pp. 76-77.

255. Dunn, "Red" John, *Perilous Trails of Texas*. *Southwestern Historical Quarterly*, Vol. XXXVI, No. 3, January 1933. P. 248.

256. Emmett, Chris, *Give Way to the Right*. *Southwestern Historical Quarterly*, Vol. XXXVIII, No. 3, January 1935. P. 232.

257. _____, *Texas Camel Tales*. *Southwestern Historical Quarterly*, Vol. XXXVII, No. 1, July 1933. Pp. 71-72.

258. Fuller, Henry C., *A Texas Sheriff*. *Southwestern Historical Quarterly*, Vol. XXXV, No. 4, April 1932. P. 334.

259. Gard, Wayne, *Frontier Justice*. *Southwest Review*, Vol. XXXV, No. 2, Spring 1950. Pp. xiv-xv.

260. Hatcher, Mattie Austin, translator, *Preliminary Studies of the Texas Catholic Historical Commission*. *Southwestern Historical Quarterly*, Vol. XXXV, No. 4, April 1932. P. 335.

261. Holden, William Curry, *The Spur Ranch: A Study of the Inclosed Ranch Phase of the Cattle Industry of Texas*. *Southwestern Historical Quarterly*, Vol. XXXVIII, No. 1, July 1934. Pp. 72-73.

262. Holland, G. A., *The Double Log Cabin*. *Southwestern Historical Quarterly*, Vol. XXXV, No. 4, April 1932. P. 334.

263. Holt, R. D., editor, *Schleicher County*. *Southwestern Historical Quarterly*, Vol. XXXV, No. 4, April 1932. P. 334.

264. Hunter, J. Marvin, *The Bloody Trail. Southwestern Historical Quarterly,* Vol. XXXV, No. 4, April 1932. P. 334.

265. Krueger, M., *Pioneer Life in Texas: An Autobiography. Southwestern Historical Quarterly,* Vol. XXXIV, No. 3, January 1931. Pp. 266-267.

266. Lake, Stuart, *Wyatt Earp: Frontier Marshal. Southwestern Historical Quarterly,* Vol. XXXVI, No. 1, July 1932. Pp. 73-74.

267. Lockhart, John Washington, *Sixty Years on the Brazos. Southwest Review,* Vol. XVII, No. 2, January 1932. Pp. vi-ix.

268. Miller, Mrs. S. G., *Sixty Years in the Nueces Valley. Southwest Review,* Vol. XVII, No. 2, January 1932. Pp. vi-ix.

269. Moore, Ike, arranger, *The Life and Diary of Reading W. Black: A History of Early Uvalde. Southwestern Historical Quarterly,* Vol. XXXVIII, No. 3, January 1935. Pp. 231-232.

270. Morgan, Jonnie R., *The History of Wichita Falls. Southwestern Historical Quarterly,* Vol. XXXV, No. 4, April 1932. P. 335.

271. Nordyke, Lewis, *Cattle Empire: The Fabulous Story of the 3,000,000 Acre XIT. Southwest Review,* Vol. XXXV, No. 1, Winter 1950. Pp. xii-xiv.

272. Osgood, Ernest Staples, *The Day of the Cattleman. Southwestern Historical Quarterly,* Vol. XXXIV, No. 2, October 1930. Pp. 177-179.

273. *The Panhandle-Plains Historical Review Volume IV.* Southwestern Historical Quarterly, Vol. XXXV, No. 4, April 1932. P. 336.

274. Poe, John W., *The Death of Billy the Kid. Southwestern Historical Quarterly*, Vol. XXXVII, No. 3, January 1934. P. 234.

275. Randolph, H. C., *Panhandle Lawyers. Southwestern Historical Quarterly*, Vol, XXXV, No. 4, April 1932. P. 335.

276. Richardson, Rupert Norval, *The Comanche Barrier to South Plains Settlement. Southwestern Historical Quarterly*, Vol. XXXVII, No. 3, January 1934. Pp. 223-224.

277. Sanger, Major D. B., *The Story of Fort Bliss. Southwestern Historical Quarterly*, Vol. XXXVIII, No. 3, January 1935. P. 233.

278. Sikes, Godfrey, *A Westerly Trend. Southwestern Historical Quarterly*, Vol. L, No. 4, April 1947. Pp. 520-523.

279. Siringo, Charles A., *Riata and Spurs. Southwestern Historical Quarterly*, Vol. XXXV, No. 4, April 1932. Pp. 333-334.

280. Smith, Tevis Clyde, *Frontier's Generation: The Pioneer History of Brown County and Surrounding Territory. Southwestern Historical Quarterly*, Vol. XXXV, No. 4, April 1932. P. 335.

281. Stapp, William Preston, *The Prisoners of Perote. Southwestern Historical Quarterly*, Vol. XXXVII, No. 3, January 1934. P. 235.

282. Thompson, Albert W., *The Story of Early Clayton, New Mexico. Southwestern Historical Quarterly*, Vol. XXXVII, No. 3, January 1934. Pp. 224-225.

283. _____, *They Were Open Range Days: Annals of a Western Frontier. Panhandle-Plains Historical Review*, Vol. XIX, 1946. Pp. 99-100.

284. *The West Texas Historical Association Yearbook Volume VII. Southwestern Historical Quarterly*, Vol. XXXV, No. 4, April 1932. P. 336.

285. *The West Texas Historical and Scientific Society Publications No. 3. Southwestern Historical Quarterly*, Vol. XXXV, No. 4, April 1932. P. 336.

MISCELLANEOUS WRITTEN MATERIAL

286. "Backward, Turn Backward," *Texas Tales*, edited for school use by David K. Sellars. Dallas and New York: Noble and Noble, 1955. Pictorial cloth. Pp. 56-58.

287. "Harold D. Bugbee," *Opening Program: The Hall of Fine Arts, Panhandle-Plains Historical Society*, Canyon: Panhandle-Plains Historical Society, May 9, 1952. Wrappers. Illustrated. P. 3.

288. "Cowboy Songs Again," *Texas and Southwestern Lore*, edited by J. Frank Dobie. Austin: University of Texas Press, 1927. Publications of the Texas Folk-Lore Society, Number VI. Pictorial wrappers. Pp. 198-205.

   A. _____, Cloth.

   B. _____, Austin: University of Texas Press and Dallas: Southern Methodist University Press; second printing, 1934. Cloth.

   "The Texas Folk-Lore Society itself had at least two different cloth bindings, one a rather light tan and another a fairly dark blue binding.

Some time later, our Press bound additional copies (of the printing, of course) and this cloth binding was somewhat of a light rust color, with a picture of the 'paisano' on the lower right front cover (the paisano was not on the covers of the TFS bindings, it originated with our Press)."

— *B. D. Kornmann, sales manager,*
Southern Methodist University Press,
Dallas, to C.A.R., February 20, 1974.

C. _____, Second printing, 1934. Green wrappers. Pages untrimmed.

D. _____, Reprint edition. Dallas: SMU Press, 1969. Cloth.

289. "A Cowman's Comment On Art," Midland: *Announcement of the Opening of Haley Ranch Gallery, Midland, Texas, March 30, 1974.* Leaflet cover is full color reproduction of Robert Lougheed's "Early Fall Snow." Pp. 2-3. Illustrated by a photo of a bronze of John Wayne by Glenna Goodacre.

290. "The Curse of Moderation," *Texans for America News,* October 1958, Vol. 1, No. 6. P. 4.

A. _____, A single page reprint.

291. "The Fallacies of the Defense of the Guidance-Counseling Program," A six-page self-mailer published and distributed by Texans for America from its headquarters at Canyon, Texas, April 21, 1961. 21cm. × 16cm.

292. "Further Deterioration In The Cause of Freedom," *Texans for America News,* Vol. I, No. 3, April 1958. Pp. 1-2.

293. "Charles Goodnight, Pioneer Cowman," *The Lone Star State, A School History* by Clarence R. Wharton. Dallas: The Southern Publishing Company, 1932. Pp. 376-378.

294. "Goodnight, Charles," *Dictionary of American Biography, Vol. 7.* New York: Charles Scribner's Sons, Copyright 1931 by American Council of Learned Societies. Pp. 393-394.

295. "Grass," *This Bitterly Beautiful Land: A Texas Common-place Book.* Compiled and edited by Al Lowman. Introduction by Carl Hertzog. Designed by William R. Holman (Roger Beacham) publisher. Austin: 1972. The leaf by J. Evetts Haley is printed on "handmade paper molded especially for this volume by the Inveresk Paper Mill in England." P. 33. 36cm. × 25cm.

296. "Judge James D. Hamlin," *Opening Program: The Hall of Fine Arts, Panhandle-Plains Historical Society,* Canyon: Panhandle-Plains Historical Society, May 9, 1952. Wrappers. Illustrated. P. 5.

297. "The Horses of the Conquest: An Appreciation of Cunninghame-Graham's Work," Reprinted from *The Cattleman,* December 1949. 4 pp. (unnumbered). 22.8cm. × 15.2cm.

298. "Horse Thieves," *Son-Of-A-Gun Stew. A Sampling of The Southwest.* Edited by Elizabeth M. Stover. Illustrations and pictorial wrapper by Harold D. Bugbee. Dallas: University Press in Dallas, Southern Methodist University, 1945. Pp. 123-137.

   A. _____, Cloth.

   "Son-Of-A-Gun Stew *was bound in both cloth and paperback at the time it was published here. Grosset & Dunlap, Inc., 51 Madison Ave., New York, New York, 10010, reprinted this title later, cloth-bound, and it certainly too must now be out of print.*"

   — B. D. Kornmann, Southern Methodist
   University Press, to C.A.R.
   February 20, 1974.

299. *The Institute of Americanism at the Texas Technological College, Lubbock.* Lubbock: Institute of Americanism, 1952. Wrappers. 4 pp. 18.2 cm. × 9.3cm.

300. "Issues and Personalities In Critical Texas Campaign," *Texans for America News,* May 1958, Vol. 1, No. 4, P. 1-2.

301. "Lasater, Edward Cunningham," *Dictionary of American Biography, Vol. 2.* New York: Charles Scribner's Sons. Copyright 1933 by American Council of Learned Societies. Pp. 12-13.

302. "Littlefield, George Washington," *Dictionary of American Biography, Vol. 11.* New York: Charles Scribner's Sons, Copyright 1933 by American Council of Learned Societies. Pp. 300-301.

303. "Lore of the Llano Estacado," *Texas and Southwestern Lore.* Austin: University of Texas Press, 1927. Publications of the Texas Folk-Lore Society, Number VI. Pictorial wrappers. Pp. 72-89.

    A.   ——————, Cloth.

    B.   ——————, Austin: University of Texas Press and Dallas: Southern Methodist Press; second printing, 1934. Cloth.

    C.   ——————, Second printing, 1934. Green wrappers. Pages untrimmed.

    D.   ——————, Reprint edition. Dallas: SMU Press, 1969. Cloth.

304. *Luziano — The Artist,* Canyon: J. Evetts Haley, 1970. Illustrated wrappers. 4 pp. 15.4cm × 22.6cm.

305. "Managing a Trail Herd," *Southwest Writers Anthology,* Martin Shockley, editor. Austin: Steck-Vaughn Co., 1967. Pp. 66-69.

306. "Mexican Mescal Mixed Well With Texans," *A Catalogue of Books, Dime Novels and Pamphlets Relating to Texas and the Southwest — Including a distinguished list of Western Illustrators, Catalogue IX.* Clarendon: Clyde I. Price, Bookseller, April 1947. Wrappers. Drawings by H. D. Bugbee, P. 2.

This humorous tale is described in the catalogue as "A fragment from the Forthcoming biography of Jeff Milton by Evetts Haley." When the biography was published, this "fragment" was not included.

307. "Now is The Time For Righteous Intolerance," *Texans for America News*, October 1958, Vol. I, No. 6. P. 3.

    A.   _____. A single page reprint, or broadside. 19cm. × 14cm.

308. "Old Blue, the Lead Steer," *A Treasury of Western Folklore*, edited by B. A. Botkin. New York: Crown Publishers, Inc., 1951. Pp. 484-487.

309. Ornduff, Donald R. *Casement of Juniata*. Kansas City, Missouri: The Lowell Press, 1975. Introduction by J. Evetts Haley. Cloth. 113 pp. Photos. Frontispiece painting of Capt. Dan D. Casement. Pictorial dust-jacket. There were 1,000 copies printed.

    A.   The "Ranch Edition." Custom bound and limited to 100 copies signed by Donald R. Ornduff and J. Evetts Haley. The edition contains a full color frontispiece portrait of Dan D. Casement. Slip-case.

> *"The bindery made the original box a trifle too small and a replacement of correct size was issued by the Lowell Press."*
> — *Donald R. Ornduff to C.A.R.*
> *January 23, 1976.*

310. "The Panhandle-Plains Historical Society's 50th Annual Meeting: The Background and Facts of a Controversy," *The Canyon News*, May 13, 1971. A full page advertisement on page 9.

311. "Pastores del Palo Duro," *Southwesterners Write* by T. M. Pearce and A. P. Thomason. Albuquerque: University of New Mexico Press, 1946. Drawings by H. D. Bugbee. Pp. 213-226.

312. "Post Mortem Of Texas Politics Points Up Sad Lessons," *Texans for America News*, October 1958, Vol. I, No. 6. Pp. 1-2.

313. "Prairie Dogs," *A Treasury of Western Folklore*, edited by B. A. Botkin. New York: Crown Publishers, Inc., 1951. Pp. 160.

314. "Report On Textbook Hearings," A six-page self-mailer issued at Canyon on November 3, 1961, and addressed to the Texans for America Committee for Education and Correspondence. 15.4cm. × 11cm.

315. "Siringo, Charles A.," *Dictionary of American Biography* Vol. 17. New York: Charles Scribner's Sons, Copyright 1935 by American Council of Learned Societies. Pp. 191-192.

316. Smedley, Betty, *Catalogue No. 11: Ranges of Grass and the men on horseback*. Austin: 1976. Wrappers. 66 pp. Printed at El Paso by Crawford-Penick, Inc. Introducton "Betty and Her Books" by J. Evetts Haley. Cover design by William D. Wittliff. Illustration by H. D. Bugbee. The front cover is a Charles M. Russell pen and ink drawing done for use as an illustration for the Program of the 40th Annual Convention of the Montana Stockgrowers Association in 1925.

317. "Strange Tales of The Llano Estacado," *Texas Tales*, edited for school use by David K. Sellars. Dallas and New York: Noble and Noble, 1955. Pictorial cloth. Pp. 110-16.

318. "Creed Taylor," *This Bitterly Beautiful Land: A Texas Commonplace Book*. Compiled and edited by Al Lowman. Austin: William R. Holman, 1972. P. 40.

319. "A Texan Looks at Lyndon," *Congressional Record*, September 1, 1964. Pp. A4550-A4551.

    A.   _____, A one-page reprint.

B. _____, A one-page reprint enlarged to 17"
× 11", with an added note by J.E.H. above an
order blank in bottom portion of the page and
photo of L.B.J. in lower lefthand corner.

C. _____, A single-page reprint, 11" × 8½",
with order blank for the book to Palo Duro Press
printed in red ink at the bottom of the page.

320. "Texans for America Endorse Candidates For State
Offices," *Texans for America News,* June-July 1958, Vol.
I, No. 5. Pp. 1-2.

321. "Texans For America Organize On State Wide Basis,"
Texans for America News, January 1958, Vol. I, No. 1.
Pp. 1-2.

322. "Texas Control of Texas Soil," A reprint from *West Texas
Today,* July 1936. 2 pp.

323. "Texas Faces Confiscation For Taxes As Income Falls,"
Texans for America News, February 1958, Vol. I, No. 2.
Pp. 1-2.

324. "To the State Committees of Correspondence and
Education, Texans for America," Canyon: Texans for
America, March 15, 1961. 4 pp. 23cm. × 18cm.

325. "Universal Military Training Vs. the Lessons of History,"
The Amarillo Register, June 17, 1955. Single page. 30cm.
× 13cm.

326. "Was Wes Hardin Shot in the Back of the Head?", *A
Treasury of Western Folklore,* edited by B. A. Botkin.
New York: Crown Publishers, Inc., 1951. Pp. 410-411.

327. "Wes Hardin Will Git You," *The Southwest in Life and
Literature,* compiled by C. L. Sonnichsen. New York:
Devin-Adair, 1962. Pp. 440-464.

328. "Gen. Albert C. Wedemeyer Suggests New Political
Party," *Texans for America News,* June 1959, Vol. II, No.
1. Pp. 1-2.

329. "What Repeal of the Poll Tax Means," A six-page self-mailer issued at Canyon on November 1, 1963, for members of *Texans for America*, 20.2cm × 15cm.

330. "Why the Political Pot Boils in Texas," Reprinted from *The Amarillo Register*, July 1, 1955. 1 p.

SOME UNPUBLISHED MANUSCRIPTS AND PAPERS

331. "Biographical Sketch of J. Evetts Haley." Canyon: 1965. 5 pp. Typewritten.

332. *Checklist of Texas Newspapers in the University of Texas Library*. Austin: University of Texas, 1933. Prepared by The Texas Historical Survey, C.W.A. Project 200111-B-11. J. Evetts Haley, director; Winnie Allen, archivist. 2 volumes. 573 pp. Typewritten.

333. "Eulogy for John Alva Haley." This eulogy. written upon the death of Evetts Haley's father, was read at the funeral service on December 31, 1937, at Midland, Texas.

334. "The Five Billions and Election in Texas." Austin: 1936. An article written during the political campaign season while Evetts was with the University of Texas. 6 pp. Typewritten.

335. *Index to Biographical Studies of Texans. Austin: University of Texas, 1935. Prepared by The Texas Historical Survey. J. Evetts Haley, director. 2 volumes. 1788 pp. Typewritten.*

336. *Index to Personal Names in Texas Gazette, Vol. I, Sept. 25, 1829 — Feb. 8, 1832.* Austin: University of Texas, 1935. Prepared by The Texas Historical Survey. J. Evetts Haley, director. 44 pp. Typewritten.

337. *Index to Personal Names in Texas Sentinel, Vol. I, Jan. 15, 1839 — Dec. 12, 1840; Vol. II, Dec. 26, 1840 — Nov. 10, 1841.* Austin: University of Texas, 1935. Prepared by The Texas Historical Survey, J. Evetts Haley, director. 162 pp. Typewritten.

338. *Key to Index To Biographical Studies of Texans 1933-1934.* Austin: University of Texas, 1935. Prepared by The Texas Historical Survey. J. Evetts Haley, director; Winnie Allen, archivist. Preface by J.E.H. 18 pp. Typewritten.

339. *List of Books Indexed by The Texas Historical Survey 1933-1934.* Austin: University of Texas, 1935. Prepared by The Texas Historical Survey, J. Evetts Haley, director. 24 pp. Typewritten.

340. *A Survey of Texas Cattle Drives to the North, 1866-1895.* Austin: J. Evetts Haley, June 1926. The thesis presented for the degree of Master of Arts at The University of Texas. 368 pp. Typewritten.

341. *A Year of Historical Exploration.* Austin: The University of Texas, 1930. 211 pp. Typewritten. Done when Evetts was collector in research in the social sciences.

EPHEMERA

342. "An April Disaster," A poem in *High, Dry and Windy,* the 1920 school annual of the Midland High School. P. 95.

343. "At Christmas." A four-page undated Christmas card from Nita and Evetts Haley printed by George Autry at Amarillo in the 1940s. The cover drawing is by Harold D. Bugbee. 11.4cm. × 15.2cm.

344. "Christmas Card." A four-page greeting, possibly issued in 1944. It is undated and the pages are unnumbered. The copy is taken from *Charles Schreiner, The Story of a Country Store.* The pen and ink drawings are by Harold Bugbee.

345. "Cow Business and Monkey Business." Reprinted by photo offset in 1975 from *The Saturday Evening Post* of December 8, 1934. There are four unnumbered pages. No date, no place of publication. Printing is on heavy white stock, reduced from original magazine size to 8½" × 11". The photo illustrations have been sharply reproduced.

346. "From the JH Ranch to You." A four-page Christmas greeting printed by George Autry at Amarillo in 1956. The cover photo of Nita and Evetts Haley was done by Edward L. Roberts. 11.4cm × 15.2cm.

347. "From the JH Ranch at Christmas." A four-page Christmas card from the press of George Autry and distributed in 1959. The photo on the upper cover is of Evetts and his favorite cutting horse, Strawberry, in the old corral. 11.4cm × 15.2cm.

348. "From Where We Still Look With Hope . . ." A single leaf Christmas greeting from Nita and J. Evetts Haley dated November 30, 1958. 13.6cm × 10.8cm.

349. "J. Evetts Haley, Candidate for Governor of Texas." Canyon: J. Evetts Haley, 1956. A four-page political fly-sheet announcing his candidacy, setting forth the issues and containing biographical material. Photo of J.E.H. in cowboy's working hat and shirt open at the throat. 20.2cm × 17.6cm.

A.   _____. A variant from which the announcement has been dropped. Photo has J.E.H. in tie and coat with formal cowboy hat. He faces left. 9cm × 20cm.

B.   _____. A variant in which J.E.H. faces right and the following notice has been added: "Please Reply To: Haley For Governor Club, Post Office Box 11177, Fort Worth, Texas."

C.   _____. A variant. The cover has been changed into a self-mailer with a small picture of J.E.H. on the left and a box for a 2¢ stamp in the upper right corner.

350. "The Heraldry of the Range." El Paso: Carl Hertzog, 1949. A sample page with order blank advertising the publication of the book. Drawing by H. D. Bugbee.

351. "The Heraldry of the Range." Text for various highway maps issued by The Shamrock Oil and Gas Corporation, Amarillo, 1947 to 1965. Drawing by H. D. Bugbee.

352. "Indian Ways and Times." Amarillo: Shamrock Oil and Gas Corporation, broadside for advertisement number 85. Illustrated by H. D. Bugbee.

353. "Jeffersonian Democrats of Texas. A Declaration." Austin: Jeffersonian Democrats of Texas, 1936. A single column fly-sheet. 22.6cm × 10cm.

354. "Labor and The New Deal." Austin: Jeffersonian Democrats of Texas, 1936. J. Evetts Haley, Chairman. Fly sheet. 22.6cm. × 10cm.

355. "On Christmas . . ." A large fold-over Christmas card hinged at the top, undated, but sent in 1967. The cover is an original oil painting by Frank Hoffman of three mustangs in a blizzard on the plains. The painting was reproduced and the card printed by George Autry at Amarillo. There are two sizes: 24.8cm × 32.6cm and 24cm × 31.2cm.

356. "The Panhandle-Plains Historical Society's 50th Annual Meeting." An eleven-page letter reproduced on J. Evetts Haley's letterhead and signed by him. It was mailed to the Board of Directors and the members of the Panhandle-Plains Historical Society. In it Haley presents his side of a controversy. Written at Canyon and dated May 10, 1971.

357. "Ranch life as it is — in some places." A poem by Evetts Haley, copyright July 1921.

358. "Regular Democrats for Landon, Texans Cite 13 Grievances Against New-Deal." A fly-sheet issued at Austin by Jeffersonian Democrats of Texas, Fall 1936.

359. "Roosevelt's Stand on Liquor and the Constitution." Austin: Jeffersonian Democrats of Texas, 1936. A two-page political advertisement featuring a cartoon by Ding Darling from the *New York Herald-Tribune.*

360. "Some Southwestern Trails." El Paso: Carl Hertzog, 1948. 4 pp. (unnumbered). A folder advertising the forthcoming publication of the book. The title page drawing is by Tom Lea.

361. "States Rights—The Issue! Interposition the Way to Preserve Them. Announcement For Governor of Texas." A political broadside issued at Canyon, February 29, 1956. 4 pp. The last page has a photo of Mr. Haley in working cowboy hat, shirt open at the neck and a short biographical sketch. 10.2cm × 22.8cm.

A. _____. A variant, the last page is blank.

362. "Earl Vandale on the Trail of Texas Books." El Paso: Carl Hertzog, 1965. A four-page announcement by the Palo Duro Press advertising publication of the book. 23.4cm × 15cm.

363. "Why Social Security Is Insecure." Austin: Jeffersonian Democrats of Texas, 1936. A fly-sheet with a cartoon by Ding Darling.

TRIVIA

364. *The Flamboyant Judge, James D. Hamlin.* The prepublication announcement printed on a dust jacket of the book and also including an order form and price list. Mailed from the Palo Duro Press, Canyon, 1973.

365. *High, Dry and Windy.* Midland: Midland High School, 1920. Evetts Haley was the athletic editor of the school annual and also contributed a poem. Living up to his motto: "Get in or get out," he was senior class president, literary society vice-president, a member of the debating club and the glee club *plus* playing quarterback on the football team.

366. "If The Range Could Talk." A six-track cassette album of old-fashioned cow country story-telling in the voice of Evetts Haley. Produced and copyrighted (1976) by The Nita Stewart Haley Memorial Library, Midland. Produced by Vick Knight. Voice introduction and editing by Robert Carr Vincent.

> *"This cassette album contains many fascinating range stories about cowboys, cowmen and their wives, peace officers, blacksmiths, merchants, windmillers, and cow-camp cooks. Even better than these are stories on their cattle and horses during the development of the fascinating frontier. Most of these stories and historical incidents of the cow country are not likely ever to be published."*
> — *Evetts Haley Jr., Midland,*
> *July 1976.*

367. *Le Mirage.* Canyon: West Texas State Teachers College, 1924 and 1925, J. Evetts Haley, editor-in-chief. Haley was president of the Class of 1923 and the Senior Class in 1925. In addition, he was editor of the *Buffalo Handbook* and columnist and business manager of *The Prairie*, the school newspaper. He was first string quarterback until a seriously injured knee forced him out of action.

368. "Panhandle-Plains Museum. At Canyon, Texas, Stands This Unique and Thorough Collection of Western Americana That Perpetuates the Old Time Cowboy, the Southwest Indian and the Land They Lived In" by Mary Whatley Clarke. *The Cattleman*, February 1961. Pp. 31-33, 48, 50. This article includes "a story told by J. Evetts Haley" about the museum's acquisition of a miniature chuck wagon from the JA Ranch.

369. "Our Constitution and Our Republic's Survival." The program for this speech at the First Congregational Church at Los Angeles, California, October 13, 1964, is printed in the *Freedom Club Bulletin* and includes several Haley quotes.

370. "El Rio Pecos, Graveyard of the Cowman's Hopes" by R. D. Holt. *The Cattleman*, July 1948. Pp. 21 et seq. The title is from a quote by J.E.H. which is used as the subtitle of the article: "The Pecos — the graveyard of the cowman's hopes. I hated it! It was as treacherous as the Indians themselves. — *Charles Goodnight, Cowman and Plainsman* by J. Evetts Haley."

371. "Some Southwestern Gift Suggestions from The Palo Duro Press." A four-page catalogue, illustrated, offering books by Haley for sale at Christmas 1969.

372. "A Texan Looks at Lyndon." A poster advertising the book. The *Congressional Record* page and front cover of the book are shown. 35cm × 28cm.

373. "A Texan Looks at Lyndon." A twelve-inch record album in illustrated jacket. It was produced for American United, Hollywood, California, and was recorded live at the 10th National Convention of "We The People" in Chicago, Illinois, September 19, 1964. The prologue is by Walter Brennan, introduction by Tom Anderson, and narrated by J. Evetts Haley. Playing time: 47 minutes.

A CHRONOLOGICAL LISTING OF THE WRITINGS OF J. EVETTS HALEY

~

1920

"An April Disaster"
(Midland, 1920)

1924

"West Texas Breezes"
(Canyon, Oct. 7, 14, 21; Nov. 4, 11, 18, 19, 24)

1925

"A Man May Be Crazy — or Merely Be Starting Toward a Big Fire"
(Canyon, Feb. 10, 1925)

"The First White Woman on the Texas Plains"
(Dallas, June 28, 1925)

"When the Panhandle Was Still Young"
(Dallas, August 2, 1925)

"The Panhandle-Plains Historical Society"
(Lubbock, September 27, 1925)

"Cowboy's Part in Plains History Was Vital"
(Amarillo, Nov. 15, 1925; Fort Worth, Dec. 1925)

"T. S. Bugbee, Second Ranchman in the Panhandle"
(Dallas, Nov. 15, 1925)

1926

A Survey of Texas Cattle Drives to the North 1886-1895
(Austin, 1926)

1927

"Cowboy Songs Again"
(Austin, 1927, 1934; Dallas, 1934, 1969)

"Lore of the Llano Estacado"
(Austin, 1927, 1934; Dallas, 1934, 1969)

Lore of the Llano Estacado; Cowboy Songs Again
(Austin, 1927)

"Historic Saddle is Saved"
(Fort Worth, January 1927)

"—And Then Came Barbed Wire To Change History's Course"
(Fort Worth, March 1927)

1928

"Charles Goodnight's Indian Recollections"
(Canyon, 1928; Bandera, December, 1928)

Charles Goodnight's Indian Recollections
(Amarillo, 1928)

1929

The XIT Ranch of Texas and the Early Days of the Llano Estacado
(Chicago, 1929; Norman, 1953; Western Frontier Library, 1967)

Burton, *A History of the JA Ranch.* (Review)
(Canyon, 1929)

"Young Cow Hands Become Old Timers"
(Fort Worth, March 1929)

"Grass Fires of the Southern Plains"
(Abilene, June 1929)

1930

"Charles Goodnight, Pioneer"
(Canyon, 1930)

A Year of Historical Exploration
(Austin, 1930)

"Portraits of the West. Harold Bugbee, Cowboy Artist, Paints the Texas Cow Camp and Trail"
(Austin, Jan.-Feb. 1930)

"Horse Thieves"
(Dallas, Spring 1930, 1945)

Osgood, *The Day of the Cattleman.* (Review)
(Austin, October 1930)

"Longhorn, Lasso and Latigo"
(New York, December 1930)

1931

"Jim East, Trail Hand and Cowboy"
(Canyon, 1931)

Jim East, Trail Hand and Cowboy
(Canyon, 1931)

"Goodnight, Charles"
(New York, 1931)

Krueger, *Pioneer Life in Texas: An Autobiography.* (Review)
(Austin, January 1931)

"The Panhandle of the Old Cowman"
(Fort Worth, February 1931)

"Cowboys Went on a Strike"
(Fort Worth, March 1931)

"Committee Visits King Ranch"
(Fort Worth, April 1931)

"Midland Historian Fans Brands of Western Literature in Talk Here; Praises The Chroniclers"
(Midland, September 11, 1931)

"Haley Discusses Old Chroniclers: Part 2"
(Midland, September 13, 1931)

"Haley Discusses Old Chroniclers: Part 3"
(Midland, September 14, 1931)

"Haley Discusses Old Chroniclers: Part 4"
(Midland, September 18, 1931)

"This Plainsman Comes Forth"
(Austin, October 1931)

1932

"Charles Goodnight, Pioneer Cowman"
(Dallas, 1932)

Moore, "A Log of the Montana Trail as Kept by Ealy Moore."
(Edited)
(Canyon, 1932; Fort Worth, February 1934)

Moore, *A Log of the Montana Trail as Kept by Ealy Moore.*
(Edited)
(Canyon, 1932)

Bell, "A Log of the Texas-California Cattle Trail, 1854." Part I
(Edited)
(Austin, January 1932)

Lockhart, *Sixty Years on the Brazos.* (Review)
(Dallas, January 1932)

Miller, *Sixty Years in the Nueces Valley.* (Review)
(Dallas, January 1932)

"The Great Plains: A New Plan for History Writing"
(Bandera, March 1932)

Bell, "A Log of the Texas-California Cattle Trail, 1854." Part II
(Edited)
(Austin, April 1932)

Bulletin of the Sam Houston State Teachers College 1931. (Review)
    (Austin, April 1932)

Canton, *Frontier Trails.* (Review)
    (Austin, April 1932)

Fuller, *A Texas Sheriff.* (Review)
    (Austin, April 1932)

Hatcher, *Preliminary Studies of the Texas Catholic Historical Commission.* (Review)
    (Austin, April 1932)

Holland, *The Double Log Cabin.* (Review)
    (Austin, April 1932)

Holt, *Schleicher County.* (Review)
    (Austin, April 1932)

Hunter, *The Bloody Trail.* (Review)
    (Austin, April 1932)

Morgan, *The History of Wichita Falls.* (Review)
    (Austin, April 1932)

The Panhandle-Plains Historical Review Volume IV. (Review)
    (Austin, April 1932)

Randolph, *Panhandle Lawyers.* (Review)
    (Austin, April 1932)

"Scouting With Goodnight"
    (Dallas, April 1932; Bandera, December 1932)

Siringo, *Riata and Spurs.* (Review)
    (Austin, April 1932)

Smith, *Frontier's Generation: The Pioneer History of Brown County and Surrounding Territory.* (Review)
    (Austin, April 1932)

The West Texas Historical Association Yearbook Vol. VII.
(Review)
    (Austin, April 1932)

The West Texas Historical and Scientific Society Publications No. 3. (Review)
    (Austin, April 1932)

Bell, *A Log of the Texas-California Cattle Trail, 1854.* Part III (Edited)
    (Austin, July 1932)

Bell, *A Log of the Texas-California Cattle Trail, 1854.* (Edited)
    (Austin, 1932)

Coolidge, *Fighting Men of the West.* (Review)
    (Austin, July 1932)

Cushing, *Zuni Folk Tales,* (Review)
    (Austin, July 1932)

Lake, *Wyatt Earp: Frontier Marshal.* (Review)
    (Austin, July 1932)

1933

Checklist of Texas Newspapers in The University of Texas Library
    (Austin, 1933)

"Lasater, Edward Cunningham"
    (New York, 1933)

"Littlefield, George Washington"
    (New York, 1933)

Dunn, *Perilous Trails of Texas.* (Review)
    (Austin, January 1933)

"News Items"
    (Austin, January 1933)

"Back-trailin' with the Old Timers"
    (Fort Worth, March 1933)

"The Great Plains History Collection"
(Austin, June 1933)

Allen, *Cowboy Lore.* (Review)
(Austin, July 1933)

"Driving A Trail Herd"
(Dallas, July 1933)

Baldwin, *Memoirs of the Late Frank D. Baldwin.* (Review)
(Austin, July 1933)

Emmett, *Texas Camel Tales* (Review)
(Austin, July 1933)

1934

"News Notes"
(Austin, January 1934)

Poe, *The Death of Billy the Kid.* (Review)
(Austin, January 1934)

Richardson, *The Comanche Barrier to South Plains Settlement.*
(Review)
(Austin, January 1934)

Stapp, *The Prisoners of Perote*
(Austin, January 1934)

Thompson, *The Story of Early Clayton, New Mexico.*
(Review)
(Austin, January, 1934)

"Pastores de Palo Duro"
(Dallas, April 1934; Albuquerque, 1946)

Pastores del Palo Duro
(Dallas, 1934)

"The Texas Historical Survey"
(Austin, April 21, 1934)

"A Glamorous Past Walks With Him. Judge Hamlin, XIT Ranch's 'South Ender,' is More Than a Man: He is History at Its Happiest"
(Abilene, May 1934)

Connelley, *Wild Bill and His Era: The Life and Adventures of James Butler Hickok.* (Review)
(Austin, July 1934)

"The Grass Lease Fight and Attempted Impeachment of the First Panhandle Judge."
(Austin, July 1934)

Holden, *The Spur Ranch: A Study of the Inclosed Ranch Phase of the Cattle Industry of Texas.* (Review)
(Austin, July 1934)

"Dave McCormick, Pioneer"
(New York, July 14, 1934)

"The Great Resoluter — Heads the Largest Chamber of Commerce In The World; It's in Texas and New Mexico"
(New York, October 1934)

"Cow Business and Monkey Business"
(Philadelphia, December 8, 1934; n.p., 1975)

"Dick Bussell, Buffalo Hunter"
(New York, December 14, 1934)

1935

Casual Comment on Current Trends
(Austin, 1935)

Index to Biographical Studies of Texans
(Austin, 1935)

Index to Personal Names in Texas Gazette Vol. I, Sept. 25, 1829 — Feb. 8, 1832
(Austin, 1935)

Index to Personal Names in Texas Sentinel Vol. I, Jan. 15, 1839 — Dec. 12, 1840; Vol. II, Dec. 26, 1840 — Nov. 10, 1841.
    (Austin, 1935)

Key to Index To Biographical Studies of Texans 1933-1934
    (Austin, 1935)

List of Books Indexed by The Texas Historical Survey 1933-1934
    (Austin, 1935)

"Siringo, Charles A."
    (New York, 1935)

"Texas Fever and the Winchester Quarantine"
    (Canyon, 1935)

Boatright, *Tall Tales of Texas Cow Camps.* (Review)
    (Austin, January 1935)

"The Comanchero Trade"
    (Austin, January 1935)

Emmett, *Give Way to the Right.* (Review)
    (Austin, January 1935)

Moore, *The Life and Diary of Reading W. Black: A History of Early Uvalde.* (Review)
    (Austin, January 1935)

Sanger, *The Story of Fort Bliss.* (Review)
    (Austin, January 1935)

"Panhandle Hopeful of Future As Plans Made for Fight on Worst Dust Storm in History"
    (Dallas, April 17, 1935)

"The Questionable Federal Bounty"
    (San Antonio, September 15, 1935)

"The Federal Menace To Education"
    (San Antonio, September 22, 1935)

"Cows in the Cotton Patch"
    (San Antonio, October 13, 1935; Abilene, November 1935; Chicago, November 3, 1935)

"Federalized Education"
    (San Antonio, October 20, 1935)

"A New Deal In Culture"
    (San Antonio, November 10, 1935; Amarillo, November 17, 1935)

1936

Charles Goodnight: Cowman and Plainsman
    (Boston, 1936; Norman, 1949)

"The Five Billions and Election in Texas"
    (Austin, 1936)

"Texas Control of Texas Soil — Shall True Texas Traditions, or a 'Philosophy of Confusion,' Make Our Politics?"
    (Abilene, July 1936)

Texas Control of Texas Soil
    (Abilene, July 1936)

The New Deal in Texas
    (Austin, October 1936)

1937

"Eulogy for John Alva Haley"
    (Midland, Dec. 31, 1937)

1938

"Last Honors Paid Pioneer Resident In Services Friday"
    (Midland, January 2, 1938)

"War on Rustlers"
    (New York, February 4, 1938)

"Benediction of Nature"
    (Amarillo, February 18, 1938)

198

"Blood on the Moon"
(Amarillo, March 26, 1938)

"Gone With The Wind"
(Amarillo, April 20, 1938)

"The Higher Cost of Higher Education"
(Amarillo, April 28, 1938)

"Sunset on the Palo Duro"
(Amarillo, May 13, 1938)

"Texian Saddles"
(Fort Worth, June 1938)

"There's Something About It"
(Amarillo, September 10, 1938)

"A State of Crisis"
(Amarillo, September 13, 1938)

"The Heritage of Nature"
(Amarillo, September 14, 1938)

"Bishop Lucey In Defence of CIO"
(Amarillo, October 7, 1938)

"The Frontiers of Freedom"
(Amarillo, October 11, 1938)

"The High Road To National Ruin"
(Amarillo, November 17, 1938)

"The Sit-Down Addicts and The Dies Committee"
(Amarillo, November 18, 1938)

"Texas Wildlife Federation Coming To The Plains"
(Amarillo, November 24, 1938)

"Possibilities of the Palo Duro"
(Amarillo, November 28, 1938)

1939

1940

"Horses"
  (Fort Worth, September 1940)

1941

1942

1943

George W. Littlefield, Texan
  (Norman, 1943, 1972, 1974)

"The Eugene C. Barker Portrait, Presentation"
  (Austin, April 1943)

The Eugene C. Barker Portrait
  (Austin, April 1943)

1944

Charles Schreiner, General Merchandise: The Story of a Country Store
  (Austin, 1944; Kerrville, 1969)

"Mrs. John A. Haley (1867-1943)"
  (Austin, April 1944)

"Back Trailing with the Old Timers. Bob Beverly — a Living Testimonial to the Encouraging Truth That Rugged Character Is Not Eroded by Time"
  (Fort Worth, May 1944)

"Letter to Walter P."
  (Austin, July 1944)

"Letter to Bailey"
  (Austin, October 1944)

1945

The University of Texas and The Issue
(Amarillo, 1945)

"People of the Plains, Bob Smith"
(Amarillo, June 3, 1945)

"People of the Plains, Fred Scott"
(Amarillo, July 15, 1945)

"People of the Plains, Colonel Jack Potter"
(Amarillo, September 9, 1945)

1946

"The Goodnight Trail"
(Canyon, 1946; Amarillo, August 1946)

"The Rath Trail"
(Canyon, 1946; Amarillo, February 1947)

Thompson, *They Were Open Range Days: Annals of a Western Frontier.* (Review)
(Canyon, 1946)

"The Cattleman Cover, Longhorns In the Buffalo Trail — Harold D. Bugbee"
(Fort Worth, October 1946)

1947

"Mexican Mescal Mixed Well With Texans"
(Clarendon, April 1947)

Sikes, *A Westerly Trend.* (Review)
(Austin, April 1947)

"The Heraldry of the Range"
(Amarillo, 1947-1965)

"The Heraldry of the Range, Some Southwestern Brands"
(Amarillo, September 1957; Duncan, Okla., March-April 1964)

"The XIT Brand"
(Amarillo, October 1947; Lubbock, November 1947; Amarillo, November 20, 1947; Dalhart, 1949)

"The Bell Ranch"
(Amarillo, November 1947)

1948

A bit of bragging about a Cow
(Amarillo, March 1948)

A Cowboy On Credit, or The Poppin' Off of a Panhandle Puncher to His Banker Friend
(El Paso, 1948)

Jeff Milton, A Good Man With a Gun
(Norman, 1948)

Some Southwestern Trails
(San Angelo, 1948; El Paso, 1948, 1949)

"The JA Ranch"
(Amarillo, January 1948)

"The 101 Brand"
(Amarillo, February 1948)

"The Matador Brand"
(Amarillo, March 1948)

"The Cross L Brand"
(Amarillo, April 1948)

"The JJ Brand"
(Amarillo, May 1948)

1949

The Heraldry of the Range, Some Southwestern Brands
(Canyon, 1949)

"Indian Ways and Times"
(Amarillo, January 1949)

"The Hide Hunt"
(Amarillo, February 1949)

"Mustangs — Wild Horses of the Plains"
(Amarillo, April 1949)

"A Day With Dan Casement"
(Kansas City, September 1, 1949)

A Day With Dan Casement
(Kansas City, September 1949)

"The Horses of the Conquest: An Appreciation of Cunninghame-Graham's Work"
(Fort Worth, December 1949)

1950

John Bouldin's first Christmas on the Plains
(Amarillo, 1950)

The Great Comanche War Trail
(Canyon, 1950; Duncan, 1964)

Gard, *Frontier Justice.* (Review)
(Dallas, Spring, 1950)

"Traveler Finds 'A Touch of Texas' Far From Home"
(Abilene, March 31, 1950)

"Little Comfort For Truman in Texas"
(San Angelo, September 3, 1950)

"Tory Talk of Mickey, Mice, and Men"
(San Angelo, September 10, 1950)

"Primary Obligation Is To The Party"
(San Angelo, September 17, 1950)

"When Mr. White Goes To Washington"
(San Angelo, October 1, 1950)

"Compulsory Education Versus Freedom"
(San Angelo, October 22, 1950)

"For High Crimes and Misdemeanors"
(San Angelo, October 29, 1950)

"Congressional Race in the Panhandle"
(San Angelo, November 5, 1950)

"Commendable Theft of Stone of Scone"
(San Angelo, November 12, 1950)

"Water, Water, But Not Everywhere"
(San Angelo, November 19, 1950)

"Just How Much Is the Dollar Worth?"
(San Angelo, November 26, 1950)

"Our Government Boards and Economy"
(San Angelo, December 10, 1950)

"Complete Mobilization Is Not The Answer"
(San Angelo, December 17, 1950)

"In Search of Unity For Our Future"
(San Angelo, December 22, 1950)

Nordyke, *Cattle Empire: The Fabulous Story of the 3,000,000 Acre XIT*. (Review)
(Dallas, Winter 1950)

1951

Casement, *The Address of Mr. Dan D. Casement at the Thirtieth Annual Meeting of the Panhandle-Plains Historical Society at Canyon, Texas, May 11, 1951*. (Edited)
(Amarillo, 1951)

"Old Blue, the Lead Steer"
(New York, 1951)

Patriotism in Our Own "Hour of Decision".
(Amarillo, 1951)

"Prairie Dogs"
(New York, 1951)

Then Came Christmas for Mildred Taitt
(Amarillo, 1951, 1962)

"Was Wes Hardin Shot in the Back of the Head?"
(New York, 1951)

Water and Power
(Canyon, 1951)

"Incipient Revolt On The High Plains"
(San Angelo, January 7, 1951)

"Mr. Truman Not Really Responsible"
(San Angelo, January 14, 1951)

"Time To Purge The United Nations"
(San Angelo, January 28, 1951)

"It's About Time To Pull In Our Horns"
(San Angelo, February 11, 1951)

"A Sorry Substitute For Diplomacy"
(San Angelo, February 18, 1951)

"On Purging The Literary Pinks"
(San Angelo, February 25, 1951)

"Price Control: The Same Old Baloney"
(San Angelo, March 11, 1951)

"Making A Mess of the Cotton Business"
(San Angelo, March 11, 1951)

"The Legislature and The University"
(San Angelo, March 25, 1951)

"Literature and the Law of Necessity"
(San Angelo, April 8, 1951)

"More Controls Only Mean Less Beef"
(San Angelo, April 15, 1951)

"The Significance Of Texas Matadors"
(San Angelo, April 25, 1951)

1952

And So it must be . . . at Christmas . . . on the ranges of grass!
   (Amarillo, 1952)

"Farewell to the Panhandle-Plains Historical Society"
   (Canyon, 1952)

Fort Concho and the Texas Frontier
(San Angelo, 1952)

The Institution of Americanism at the Texas Technological College, Lubbock
   (Lubbock, 1952)

Life on the Texas Range
   (Austin, 1952, 1973)

"Harold D. Bugbee"
   (Canyon, May 9, 1952)

"Judge James D. Hamlin"
   (Canyon, May 9, 1952)

Americanism Without Apology
   (Wichita Falls, October 20, 1952)

1953

Christmas at the Hancock House
   (Amarillo, 1953)

1954

Story of the Shamrock
   (Amarillo, 1954)

"The Quest for Story Material"
   (Portales, June 10, 1954)

1955

"Backward, Turn Backward"
   (Dallas and New York, 1955)

"Harold D. Bugbee, Western Artist"
(Amarillo, 1955)

"Strange Tales of The Llano Estacado"
(Dallas and New York, 1955)

Those Who Came Before Us . . . caught for all time by the brush of Harold D. Bugbee
(Lubbock, 1955)

What The Teachers Think of Education. A Survey of Faculty Opinion at Texas Technological College, Lubbock, Texas
(Lubbock, 1955)

"Universal Military Training Vs. the Lessons of History"
(Amarillo, June 17, 1955)

"Why The Political Pot Boils in Texas"
(Amarillo, July 1, 1955)

"Focus on the Frontier"
(Amarillo, Sept.-Oct. 1955)

"Christmas on The Range"
(Amarillo, Nov.-Dec. 1955)

"Huffman and the Montana Cow Country"
(Amarillo, Nov.-Dec. 1955)

1956

Some Problems of Museum Board Relationships
(Canyon, 1956)

"Texas Great Plains Country"
(Amarillo, Spring 1956)

"Interposition and States Rights"
(Amarillo, June 21, 1956)

"All in the Day's Work"
(Amarillo, Summer 1956)

"Adventurous Lens of Erwin Smith"
(Amarillo, Fall 1956)

"Work and Play on the Range"
(Amarillo, Winter 1956)

1957

Focus on the Frontier
(Amarillo, 1957)

When The Stagecoach Ruled The Road
(Wichita, 1957)

"The Last Great Chief"
(Amarillo, Spring 1957)

"Marcy — Explorer"
(Amarillo, Summer, 1957)

"Buffalo Hunter"
(Amarillo, Fall 1957)

1958

Ode to Nita by Her Husband
(Canyon, 1958)

"Texans For America Organize On State Wide Basis"
(Fort Worth, January 1958)

"Texas Faces Confiscation For Taxes As Income Falls"
(Fort Worth, February 1958)

"Further Deterioration In The Cause of Freedom"
(Fort Worth, April 1958)

"R. S. Mackenzie, Indian Fighter"
(Amarillo, Spring 1958)

"Issues and Personalities In Critical Texas Campaign"
(Fort Worth, May 1958)

"Texans For America Endorse Candidates For State Offices"
(Fort Worth, June-July 1958)

"Ab Blocker, Trail Boss"
(Amarillo, Summer 1958)

"The Curse of Moderation"
(Fort Worth, October 1958)

"L'Archeveque, the Outlaw"
(Amarillo, Fall 1958)

"Now is the Time For Righteous Intolerance"
(Fort Worth, October 1958)

"Post Mortem Of Texas Politics Points Up Sad Lessons"
(For Worth, October 1958)

"John Bouldin's first Christmas on the Plains"
(Amarillo, Christmas 1958)

"Yesteryear's Christmas With The Cowboys"
(Amarillo, Christmas 1958)

1959

Erle P. Halliburton, Genius With Cement
(Duncan, 1959)

"Ben Ficklin, Pioneer Mail Man"
Amarillo, Spring 1959)

"Gen. Albert C. Wedemeyer Suggests New Political Party"
(Fort Worth, June 1959)

"Martha Summerhayes, Frontier Army Wife"
(Amarillo, Summer 1959)

"Ray C. Johnson, Gentleman and Lawyer"
(Amarillo, Fall 1959)

"Christmas at the Hancock House"
(Amarillo, Christmas 1959)

1960

Moon, *Textbook Criteria For Young Americans.* (Edited)
(Fort Worth and El Paso, 1960)

F. Reaugh, Man and Artist
(El Paso, 1960)

"Santanta, the Orator of the Plains"
(Amarillo, Spring 1960)

"F. Reaugh, Man and Artist"
(Amarillo, Summer 1960)

"Hank Smith, Frontier Settler"
(Amarillo, Fall 1960)

1961

Christmas in Palo Duro. A Repellant World — Warmed by the Spirit
(Amarillo, 1961)

Painting and Prejudice — A Comment on the Nature of Cultivated Degeneracy
(El Paso, 1961)

"To the State Committees of Correspondence and Education, Texans for America"
(Canyon, March 15, 1961)

"General Grenville M. Dodge, Builder of Railroads"
(Amarillo, Spring 1961)

"The Fallacies of the Defense of the Guidance-Counseling Program"
(Canyon, April 21, 1961)

"Andrew Jackson Potter, Fighting Parson"
(Amarillo, Summer 1961)

"John R. Baylor, Irrepressible Rebel"
(Amarillo, Fall 1961)

"Report on Textbook Hearings"
    (Canyon, November 3, 1961; Fullerton, 1961)

1962

"Wes Hardin Will Git you"
    (New York, 1962)

"Charlie Siringo, Cowboy Chronicler"
    (Amarillo, 1962)

"Testimony of J. Evetts Haley"
    (Austin, May 31, 1962)

"Bill Greene of Cananea Copper"
    (Amarillo, Summer 1962)

"Dad Joiner, Wildcatter"
    (Amarillo, Fall 1962)

1963

Men of Fiber
    (El Paso, 1963)

"Charles Schreiner, Pioneer Merchant"
    (Amarillo, Spring 1963)

"Bob Beverly, Cowboy Sheriff"
    (Amarillo, Summer 1963)

"John Armstrong, Texas Ranger"
    (Amarillo, Fall 1963)

"What Repeal of the Poll Tax Means"
    (Canyon, November 1, 1963)

"Cowboy Sheriff"
    (Midland, December 1963)

1964

A Texan Looks At Lyndon, A Study in Illegitimate Power
    (Canyon, 1964)

"The Butterfield Trail"
(Duncan, March-April 1964)

"The Marcy Trail"
(Duncan, March-April 1964)

"Jim Cook, On The Frontiers of Fantasy"
(Amarillo, Spring 1964)

"Up the Potomac Without a Paddle"
(Nasville, April 1964)

"Erle P. Halliburton, Cementer"
(Amarillo, Summer 1964)

"A Texan Looks at Lyndon"
(Washington, September 1, 1964; Canyon, September 1964)

"Our Constitution and Our Republic's Survival"
(Los Angeles, October 13, 1964)

1965

McGowan, *The Jury — Barrier to Tyranny*. (Edited)
(Canyon, 1965)

Oden, *Early Days on the Texas-New Mexico Plains*. (Edited)
(Canyon, 1965)

Earl Vandale on the Trail of Texas Books
(Canyon, 1965)

"The Constitution and its Betrayal"
(Tulsa, September 30, 1965)

1966

"The Making of a Scout"
(Austin, May-June 1966)

1967

"A Texan Still Looks At Lyndon"
(Washington, January 6, 1967)

"Managing a Trail Herd"
(Austin, 1967)

1968

Frame, "Is This the Rockefeller Blueprint designed to destroy the Reagan Movement in your state?" (Edited)
(Fort Worth, January 15, 1968)

Pike, "Albert Pike's Journeys in the Prairie 1831-1832" (Edited)
(Canyon, 1968)

1969

Mullin, *The Strange Story of Wayne Brazel.* (Introduction)
(Canyon, 1969)

Pike, *Albert Pike's Journeys in the Prairie, 1831-1832.* (Edited)
(Canyon, 1969)

Edmondson, "E. Irving Couse — Painter of Indians" (Edited)
(Canyon, 1969)

1970

Luziano — The Artist
(Canyon, 1970)

"Charles Goodnight: Pioneer Cattleman"
(Oklahoma City, Summer 1970)

1971

"The Panhandle-Plains Historical Society's 50th Annual Meeting"
(Canyon, May 10, 1971)

1972

The Flamboyant Judge, James D. Hamlin. (with William Curry Holden)
(Canyon, 1972)

"Grass"
(Austin, 1972)

"Creed Taylor"
(Austin, 1972)

1973

Robbing Banks Was My Business, The Story of J. Harvey Bailey, America's Most Successful Bank Robber
(Canyon, 1973)

1974

"A Cowman's Comment On Art"
(Midland, March 30, 1974)

The Alamo Mission Bell
(Austin, 1974)

1975

Ornduff, *Casement of Juniata* (Introduction)
(Kansas City, 1975)

"Introduction of Mr. Rarick"
(Amarillo, March 18, 1975)

1976

Smedley, *Catalogue No. 11: Ranges of Grass and The Men On Horseback* (Introduction)
(Austin, 1976)

Rough Times — Tough Fiber
(Canyon, 1976)

Ranges of Grass and the men on horseback
(Canyon, 1976)

To The Cowboy Artists of America
(Canyon, 1976)

INDEX

~

Authors Titles Item Numbers

If an item has subclassifications, only the principal assigned number is shown. Short titles are used in some instances.

A

B

C

D

E

I

M

N

Q

R

S

T

X

Y

Z

VITAE OF
CONTRIBUTING AUTHORS

MELVIN E. BRADFORD, the author of "The Care and Keeping of Memory: J. Evetts Haley and Plutarchian Biography," is a prolific writer, scholar, acadamician, teacher, researcher, bibliographer and practical politician. Born in Fort Worth, Texas, on May 8, 1934, he is married and has one son. In 1955, he graduated from the University of Oklahoma at Norman with a bachelor's degree and was awarded his master's in 1956. He received the Doctor of Philosophy degree from Vanderbilt University in 1968.

Doctor Bradford began his career as an officer instructor in English at the United States Naval Academy at Annapolis from 1957 to 1959. His term at Annapolis was preceded by a year at sea with the Navy as a Flag Lieutenant. He is presently a member of the U.S. Naval Reserve on inactive status.

Additionally, he was a Fellow at Vanderbilt University from 1959 to 1962; assistant and associate professor in English, and Head, at Hardin-Simmons University, 1962-1964; assistant professor, Northwestern State College of Lousiana, 1964-1967; assistant professor in English at the University of Dallas, 1967-1969, and associate professor in Politics and Literature at the same institution in 1969. From January, 1970 to August, 1973, he was Chairman of the Department of English at the University of Dallas, and since then has been Head of the Department.

Active in politics throughout most of his adult life, he has served as State Democratic Committeeman for the 8th District of Texas since 1972.

Articles and esays by Mel Bradford have been published in Europe and America. Among the books and periodicals in which his work has appeared are *Southern Review, Georgia*

Review, Modern Age, Triumph, Sewanee Review, Mississippi Quarterly, University Bookman, A Bibliographical Guide to the Study of Southern Literature, Louisiana Studies, South Atlantic Quarterly, Writing in English (Tokyo), Studies in Short Fiction, The Form Discovered: Essays on the Achievement of Andrew Lytle, Religion and Society, Southern Humanities Review, Arlington Quarterly, The Short Fiction of Caroline Gordon, National Review, Recherches Anglaises et Americaines (France), Contemporary Novelists, Southwestern American Literature, American Literature and the Bicentennial, The Southern Tradition at Bay, The Freeman, Presbyterian Journal, Forum, and Papers in English Language and Literature.

There is a long list of essays scheduled for publication in 1975, two of which have J. Evetts haley's writing as the subjects. Forthcoming from the University of Dallas Press are two books on Faulkner: Faulkner's Doctrine of Nature and Of Pride and Humility: Studies in Faulkner's Short Fiction.

Dr. Bradford was appointed to the editorial board of Modern Age in May, 1970, and to the board of Occasional Review in June, 1973. Also in 1970, he received a National Endowment for the Humanities Grant and gave the Redmond lectures at Hampden-Sydney on Faulkner's Reivers and Southern folklore. In 1972, he attended the Robert A. Taft Institute on Contemporary Government and the Gulf Coast Research Conference. Among the numerous addresses and papers he has delivered, two in 1973 are worthy of note here: the John C. Calhoun Memorial Address at the University of South Carolina, and the Western American Literature Association Address on J. Evetts Haley.

Of special interest to followers of Evetts Haley is the publication of A Bibliographical Guide to Southwestern American Literature by The Swallow Press of Chicago in 1977. Dr. Bradford has written sections on Haley and E. E. Dale. There is also a section on history and politics in the region written in collaboration with Dr. John Alexander Carroll.

GERRY BURTON, who wrote Haley: He's Known It All, was born Geraldine Marie Wolf on March 31, 1928 in Floresville, Texas. She attended Floresville public schools and Southwest

Texas State Teachers College, majoring in English. Gerry is married to J. C. Burton Jr. The couple have two sons, John Bryan and Robert Michael, and one granddaughter, Bryana Kay. She is presently a member of the staff of the *Lubbock Avalanche-Journal*. Previous employers include the *Abilene Reporter News* and the *Snyder Daily News*.

Mrs. Burton's main avocations are photography and the pursuit of the history of West Texas. She is a member of the Scurry County Historical Survey Committee and the Ranch Headquarters Association.

"My avid interest in history," she relates, "began in Scurry County where pioneers were still around to talk of cattle drives, nesters, range wars, and so on. I tramped the countryside to find and log historic sites, and in the process met many of those who knew the wild days in the brakelands of the caprock where everything ever told about the West in the fantasyland of motion pictures actually happened.

"I learned to love the look in tired eyes and seamed faces that talked about 'things western' when the land was open and men fought for it."

JOHN A. HALEY, who write from a deep understanding of his subject, displays a kinship with nature that can only have come from countless hours in the saddle with the herd, riding fence, or purely for pleasure. He writes to the point, without superfluous padding, right from the heart. He has made "He Is A Cowboy" interesting and easily understandable to those who have never ridden his trail.

John Haley was born August 16, 1926, at Midland, Texas, and has spent most of his life on ranches. His parents, John Furman Haley and Florence M. (Trent) Haley, were married on December 1, 1924, and lived on a small ranch in eastern Loving County that his father had traded for in 1915. John A. and his family now live on this same place, "a gift from Daddy several years ago," he relates, and raise Charolais crossbred cattle. It may be that there's a strain in the Haley genes that makes them good cowboys, and good writers. There is no question that they have more than the normal amount of intestinal fortitude, which holds true in John's case, too. Sometimes it takes a lot of guts to admit to being the nephew of J. Evetts Haley!

CARL HERTZOG has been in Texas more than half-a-century working as a printer, an advertising promoter, and in business for himself. For 25 years he was the Director of Texas Western Press at the University of Texas at El Paso.

Jean Carl Hertzog was born in Lyons, France, on February 8, 1902. His parents were American students studying abroad. Carl attended schools from the first grade through college in Pittsburgh, Pennsylvania. He arrived in El Paso in June, 1923, and worked as a printer until 1927 when he went into advertising for a woodwork manufacturer based in El Paso but with national distribution. In 1930, he joined a banknote company where he learned lithography and experimented with the photo-litho process. He again joined his first employer, The McNath Company, in 1933, before starting his own business in 1934. Carl describes this venture as "started on a shoe-string, pitifully under-equipped." He expanded the business to a partnership in 1944 and sold out in 1948 to join the faculty of the University of Texas at El Paso. He started the Texas Western Press at UTEP in 1951 and acted as its director until his retirement in 1972. He is now a free lance designer and patron of the Library at UTEP.

SAVOIE LOTTINVILLE, a native of Hagerman, Idaho, which is, as he proudly asserts, "a part of the Great West," was for thirty-five years Director of the University of Oklahoma Press and for five additional years Regents Professor of History in the University of Oklahoma. He holds degrees from that University, Oxford (B.A. and M.A.) and the Litt. D. and D. Hum, the former from Southern Methodist University and the latter from Coe College.

Dr. Lottinville is the author of *The Rhetoric of History*, recently published by the University of Oklahoma Press, and is the editor of Paul Wilhelm, Duke of Wurttemberg, *Travels in North America, 1822-1823*, and George Bent, *Life of George Bent Written from His Letters by George E. Hyde*, and the co-editor (with Robert V. Hine) of *Soldier in the West: Letters of Theodore Talbot During His Services in California, Mexico, and Oregon, 1845-1853*, all published by Oklahoma. He is presently editing Thomas Nuttall's *Arkansas-Oklahoma Journal of 1818-1819*, a travel account by the great Yorkshire naturalist who, without degrees of any kind, lent distinction to Harvard for a decade or more.

AL LOWMAN, the contributor of "A Bookman's View of J.E.H.," is a native Texan who grew up and still lives on the family ranch near San Marcos. He attended local public schools and the University of Texas at Austin, earning his B.A. and M.A. degrees. Currently he is a research associate on the staff of the University of Texas Institute of Texas Cultures at San Antonio. Al has long been interested in Western history, folklore, and art, and his pursuit of books on these subjects has resulted in three exceptionally fine publications, now much sought after by collectors: *This Bitterly Beautiful Land: A Texas Commonplace Book, Printer at the Pass: The Work of Carl Hertzog,* and *Printing Arts in Texas*

Articles by Al Lowman have appeared in *Texas Libraries, Southwestern Art,* and *Arizona and the West;* his book reviews in *Southwestern Historical Quarterly.* He wrote the introduction for the catalogue of Tom Lea's paintings exhibited at San Antonio in late 1969. Additionally, Al wrote the text and researched *125 Years of Methodism in San Marcos,* designed by William Holman with drawings by both E. M. Schiwetz *and* Jose Cisneros.

Lowman is a member of the Texas Committee for the Humanities and Public Policy, the Western History Association, and the Texas State Historical Association in which he holds honorary life membership — the highest distinction conferred by that organization.

JOHN L. McCARTY, author of "Some Memories of H. D. Bugbee," was born in Bell County in 1901, and was reared at Abernathy, on the Hale-Lubbock county line, where he starred in track and field events, as well as debate and spelling. He started his newspaper career with the old *Abernathy Breeze* and broke horses for extra cash while in high school. In 1924 he graduated from West Texas State University with a bachelor's degree, and earned his master's thesis in 1942.

Mr. McCarty joined the old *Amarillo Tribune* staff in 1923 and the following year started work for the *Amarillo Globe.* He was editor and publisher of the *Dalhart Texan* from 1929 to

1936, at which time he returned to Amarillo and worked for the *Globe-News* as editor and associate publisher until 1948. At that point, he opened an insurance office and public relations firm.

Mr. McCarty was a noted author with a number of books to his credit. Best known were *Maverick Town, the story of Old Tascosa* and *Adobe Walls Bride, the story of Billy and Olive Dixon.* He always considered his finest writing to be the last chapter of *Maverick Town,* entitled "How a Town Dies."

At one time, he was concessionaire at Palo Duro Canyon State Park, and in 1952 was elected chairman of the Potter County Democratic executive committee. He was president of the Estate Life Insurance Company and the Estate Development Company in the mid-1950s.

Mr. McCarty began his professional art career in 1958 with the late George M. Autry and studied under Dord Fitz. He held a one-man art show at the Burr Galleries in New York City in 1960. A prolific artist, often working 16 hours a day, he is also known for his development of artists, including Carl Smith of Canyon and Kenneth Wyatt of Tulia. For years Mc-Carty was considered an authority on art, artists and the art world and was often asked to place a value on paintings either as investments or for insurance purposes.

He was past president of the Rotary Clubs at Amarillo and Dalhart, and of the Panhandle Press Association. He also was a member of the Panhandle Plains Historical Society, the Texas Philosophical Society and the Texas Institute of Letters. A Mason, he was a member of the Scottish Rite and Knights Templar, and a past potentate of the Khiva Temple of the Shrine.

At the time of his death on September 16, 1974, he was owner of the High Plains Art Gallery, established in 1960, and earlier that month had opened another gallery at Las Tiendas in Amarillo.

~

RICHARD M. MOOREHEAD has written numerous pieces about Evetts Haley's career including one excellent profile about his campaign for governor. His "Textbook Tempest" series in *The Dallas Morning News* won praise from the public and the State Board of Education.

Mr. Moorehead was born in Plainview, Texas, on November 16, 1913. Like Haley, he is proud of his West Texas breeding. After attending local schools, he went to Wayland College, the University of Missouri and The University of Texas from which he graduated in 1935 with a degree in journalism.

Serving his apprenticeship with the *Plainview Herald*, he worked a short time for the United Press (now UPI) before joining *The Dallas Morning News* staff at Austin in 1942. He has been Bureau Chief there since 1965. In an illustrious career he has covered national and state political conventions of both major parties, as well as the statehouse, and is a journalist-member of the Texas Civil Judicial Council. Among the organizations to which he belongs are local and national journalism societies, Association of Petroleum Writers, and the Presbyterian Church.

The writing of Mr. Morehead has been honored with awards by the Austin Headliners Club, United Press Association, State Bar of Texas and Southwestern Journalism Forum of Southern Methodist Universit. He has co-authored several books on race relations and state government, and, with Mrs. Morehead, wrote the popular "Texas Wild Game Cook Book."